Amazing Encounters with God

"Clayton shows us ways…to train our eyes and ears and hearts to identify the voice of God as He speaks to us through the people we live and work with and the conversations and interactions we have every single day."

David Nasser
Author
Pastor of Christ City Church, Birmingham, Alabama

m Boles

Amazing Encounters with God

Clayton King

HARVEST HOUSE PUBLISHERS

EUGENE, OREGON

Cover by Left Coast Design, Portland, Oregon

Back-cover author photo © Bob Carey

Clayton King's agent: David Van Diest of the Van Diest Literary Agency, PO Box 2385, Redmond, OR 97756

AMAZING ENCOUNTERS WITH GOD

Published by Harvest House Publishers
Eugene, Oregon 97402
www.harvesthousepublishers.com

Library of Congress Cataloging-in-Publication Data

King, Clayton, 1972-
Amazing encounters with God / Clayton King.
p. cm.
Expanded ed. of: Surrounded by the sacred. 2009.
ISBN 978-0-7369-3776-4 (pbk.)
1. Christian life. 2. King, Clayton, 1972- I. King, Clayton, 1972- Surrounded by the sacred. II. Title.
BV4501.3.K553 2011
248.4—dc22

2010022205

Printed in the United States of America

11 12 13 14 15 16 17 18 19 / LB-NI / 10 9 8 7 6 5 4 3 2

In honor of my parents and grandparent, aunts and uncles, who taught me the value and importance of telling stories around the table and the fireplace.

Thanks

A guy like me doesn't just decide to sit down and write a book, no matter how much natural ability I may have been granted. There are people to blame, culpability to be doled out, individuals who must be held accountable for helping awaken in me the love for literature, history, theological reflection, and, in its simplest form, the art and discipline of writing. Here are the culprits:

To my three high-school English teachers, Mrs. Tracy, Mrs. Knipple, and Mr. Evans: A huge thank-you for pushing me in the honors program all the way through to my advanced-placement exam, and for demanding more from me than I would have done without your encouragement and chastisement.

To my professors Dr. Still, Dr. Canoy, and Dr. Stacy: Your intellectual approach to theology was never greater than your faithful approach to Jesus, and you opened a treasure chest for me when you taught me to see what God was up to in this world and how I could notice His activity if I would discipline myself to see it.

To my mentors Doug Murphy, Ronnie Powell, Jake Thornhill, and Wilkes Skinner: Only in eternity will you know how much your care and your examples helped shape me for ministry.

To my closest friends (here we go!): Matt Orth, Brian Burgess, Perry Noble, Steven Furtick, J.D. Greear, Jonathan Martin, Johnnie Moore, Bruce Ashford, Seth Stevens, Jeremy Berger, Justin Brock, Brad Borders, Derwin Gray, Nathan Smith, Mac Powell, David Nasser, Scott Ray, and Bubba Thurman...I cannot believe I have this many best friends. I am wealthy in friendship if in nothing else.

To Mama and Daddy: All that I am in this life is because you loved me and showed me Jesus. You stuck with each other through thick and thin, and one day I look forward to seeing you in heaven, where there will be no more sickness or sorrow.

And to my dearest Charie, mother of my boys and keeper of my affection and love: What would I do without my Liddy? You are the single most wonderful thing in my life. I love you with all my heart and soul.

Contents

Just One Breath Away

I LIVE BY A HANDFUL OF UNSHAKABLE CONVICTIONS—or at least I try to. These convictions affect what I believe about my family, my calling, the world around me, and the people who inhabit this world.

One is that my marriage to my wife is more about making me holy than making me happy, so by God's grace we'll remain married no matter what life throws at us. Another is that it's my joy and responsibility, along with my wife, to raise our children to know Jesus, tell the truth, work hard, have compassion, and treat everyone with respect.

These convictions, like a road map, guide my everyday life and decisions. If they were anything other than unshakable, I couldn't build my life on them. Convictions have to be firm, like a rock. They have to be solid enough, like the foundation of a home, to handle the heavy construction, not to mention the storms that will test that construction over the days and years and decades.

The unshakable conviction that has led me through the crafting of this book is a simple one, one that you will hear over and over again on these pages: *We are constantly in the presence of God* as He speaks to us through the everyday occurrences of life, and when He uses ordinary things to show us Himself, we see that we are always just one breath away from an encounter with Him.

That conviction not only guides this book; it also drives my life. God is active and alive and near to us. He's not an outer-space god. He's always speaking to the human race, always revealing His character and personality and love and grace through the stuff we usually ignore and stumble over. If we are willing to listen, He will tune our hearts and minds to His message.

> God...is never far from you. He is close, maybe as close as the next person you meet, the next song you hear, or the next conversation you have.

Once you learn how to look, you'll be surprised to find that His presence is everywhere, all the time, coming at you from every direction—sometimes like a tornado that knocks you off your feet, sometimes like a flash of lightning that takes your breath away, and sometimes like a small child who leaps from behind a door to surprise his jumpy dad (not that this has ever happened to me).

Some call this theological reflection. Others call it spiritual discernment. I like to call it "paying attention." God is everywhere. Sometimes He's screaming at us to get our attention before we make a life-altering mistake in a relationship. Other times He whispers to us as we drive to work or school, letting us know we are forgiven even for sins we have forgotten. He can gently nudge us by using a lyric in a worship song we heard at just the right time, or He can smack us upside the head because we were too preoccupied with selfish things to listen to Him when He wanted to whisper. One way or another, He's going to get our attention. All of nature and life is at His disposal.

That is what we are up to here, in this book, on these pages. I want to remind you just how accessible God is to you. I want to show you that you don't need a seminary degree to experience His presence yourself. I also intend to argue that ordinary, regular, run-of-the-mill people can have some life-changing encounters with God in the most random and mundane places. You can come to grasp things about God that you never saw in Scripture, never heard about in church, or totally missed as a teenager, just by learning the discipline of paying attention to your life.

It's easy once you realize you're already swimming in sacred waters. The earth is God's. All truth is God's truth. All beauty reflects the glory of God. And He can and does employ whatever means He wants to teach you and me what He wants to teach us because, after all, the world is His. This means *everything* obeys His command—so if He decides to unleash the power of the wind, a song, a scene in a movie, or a kind word from a stranger at the market, He will.

What would you think if I told you that one of the best sermons I ever preached was inspired by watching a Guns N' Roses concert on television? And that an Italian World War II veteran taught me about forgiveness on an airplane? Or that a drunken millionaire showed me how to look past people's outer appearances and look instead into their hearts? Or that an epiphany on the way to preschool with my four-year-old made me break down so badly I could barely see through my tears to drive? You have had dozens, if not hundreds, of amazing encounters with God whether you knew it or not.

May you never miss another such moment; may you be looking for God when He reveals Himself to you next time. And the next, and the next.

The pages that follow will not distract you from God's Word. They will illuminate it, reinforce it, and make it come alive in a new way for you. When you can't reach for your Bible, or your favorite Christian radio station isn't playing in the background, or you find yourself far removed from your Sunday-morning worship service, you can still see

God. You can still hear God. You can still feel God. He is never far from you. He is close, maybe as close as the next person you meet, the next song you hear, or the next conversation you have.

So keep your ears open and your eyes peeled. His presence could be as close as your next breath.

1

Set Apart

Paul, a servant of Christ Jesus, called to be an apostle and set apart for the gospel of God.

—Romans 1:1

My personal office—my study—lies mostly underground, in the basement of my home. I go there to flesh out the ideas and inspirations that assault me during the day. It's there that I practice theological reflection, the art of seeing the sacred that constantly surrounds me... and my basement study is one of the few places I can be alone, quiet, still, and focused.

My study looks like me. I've surrounded myself in that space with things that reflect my personality and my history: Action figures line the top of my bookshelf; thousands of volumes of theology, history, biography, and fiction fill the walls; and my bearskin rug is conspicuously displayed as a testimony to my deep love for the sport of hunting. But there's one certain item in my study that to me is simply priceless and irreplaceable.

It's a glass Coca-Cola bottle.

What makes this bottle so special is not the type of glass, its design, or the factory it was produced in. What makes it so special is the person it belonged to before it fell into my hands.

What would make a Coke bottle sacred? What makes anything sacred? What processes have to take place before a person, a place, or a moment in time is considered holy? And beyond that, what do the words *sacred* and *holy* even mean? They're used often enough, but I get the feeling that the average person has no real understanding of such spiritual-sounding words. I know they've always sounded a bit intimidating to me. But I think the glass Coke bottle that adorns my study shelf might serve as a simple lesson on what makes something sacred.

God Himself is the One who does the setting apart. It's nothing but His touch that makes the person, the object, or the day sacred.

The word *holy* simply means "set apart." At least that is the easiest and most common definition. Instead of what we usually think of when we hear that word (visions from the book of Revelation of angels, thrones, scrolls, and bowls), "holy" is a simple word with a history to it. In order for something to be "set apart," some questions need to be asked.

1. Who set the thing apart?
2. What was the purpose for this setting apart?

In the Scriptures we see that God Himself is the One who does the setting apart. It's nothing but His touch that makes the person, the object, or the day sacred. If *I* declare something sacred, it means nothing. I might as well declare myself the president of the United States. Such a declaration is meaningless because I lack the authority to make it, and I also lack the innate holiness to transfer onto someone or something to make it, or them, holy.

God, on the other hand, is already holy and sacred. He is, within His own nature, set apart from us (though He did become one of us in Jesus Christ). So God is the sole power and person in all the created order of the universe who has the right, the power, and the authority to deem something sacred and holy. It's His touch that sets something apart.

Life is filled with sacred moments inhabited by God and ordained by God; they show us who He is and transform us into His people who know Him and love Him. He is holy, and when He touches a moment we are caught up in, it becomes sacred to us because God Himself was present. Our task is to train our eyes and ears to notice the "holiness" of average moments and average things—conversations with strangers, scenes in movies, lyrics in a song.

So what about the Coke bottle?

For 18 years I prayed relentlessly that God would do one thing for me: I wanted to meet Billy Graham. I began asking God for this when I was 14 years old, right after I became a Christian and surrendered my life to the very strong calling I felt to preach the gospel. Billy Graham was the most recognizable Christian face on the planet, history's greatest ambassador of the gospel, and in 1987 when I converted to faith, he was at the height of his global crusade ministry.

Needless to say, I was told to forget it. Everyone said there was no way on earth I would ever meet him.

This was the line I was given for nearly 20 years. At first, he was too busy. Then as I entered college, I was told he was focusing on his last stretch of crusades in major American cities before he was too old to continue his strenuous schedule. Then I was told his health was failing and he wasn't able to meet new people; he was being protected from all requests like mine. All of this made perfect sense, and I was impressed with the level of loyalty and professionalism his organization displayed. But I wasn't content to take no for an answer.

Through a series of crazy events, and with the help of a few friends who knew Mr. Graham, my prayers were finally answered on April 15, 2005. His public preaching ministry had ended because of his failing health, and he was spending most of his time at his home in Montreat, North Carolina, with his wife, Ruth.

I'd become friends with a student at a local university. We met during a skeet-shooting outing, and I found out he lived at Montreat. Of course, the first question I asked was, "Have you ever met Billy Graham or seen him around there?"

With an easy grin, he nonchalantly said, "Of course I have. I grew up with his grandkids and spent the summer swimming in his pool."

Several months later, my wife and I were visiting my new friend in Montreat on a Sunday afternoon when his father, Mr. Graham's personal doctor, made a visit to the Graham home. He invited us to tag along in the car. The next thing I knew, we were sitting inside the home of my hero in the faith, the man I admired and loved for his simplicity and integrity.

God is speaking to us and touching us all the time, and we are most often too busy to even notice His attempts to get our attention.

I would love to tell you every word of the three-hour conversation we had that afternoon, and I could, because I've recorded all of it in a notebook that I keep in a safe place. But as you know, this is about a Coke bottle.

When we sat down in the living room, one of Mr. Graham's assistants asked us if we wanted anything to eat or drink. He gave us a list of options to choose from: ice cream, root-beer float, water, juice, and so on. My wife and I both decided to have a root-beer float. (For the record, he could have given me liquefied tar and I wouldn't have known the difference. I was too overcome with emotion to notice.) Our friend and his father asked for a soft drink. But when Mr. Graham was asked, he responded by saying, "I will have a Coca-Cola."

About an hour later Mr. Graham excused himself to go check on Ruth. As he moved slowly away holding onto his walker, I was eyeballing the half-empty Coke bottle sitting beside his chair. I asked the assistant what he planned to do with it, and he said he was going to throw it away. I declared it would be a serious tragedy to discard such a priceless item and have it tossed into a landfill, since someone who knew its true worth could easily rescue it and treasure it as their most prized possession.

Evidently, I made a case for sparing the bottle. When we left later that afternoon, not only did I have my picture taken with Mr. Graham, and not only did he inscribe my Bible, but I left his log cabin on the top of Piney Cove with an empty Coca-Cola bottle stuck inconspicuously under my arm.

That item now holds a place of high honor in my study and in my heart. It affords me more than just an opportunity to tell a good story. It brings me back to a time when I was in the presence of a holy man—one of the greatest moments of my life. In itself, the bottle has no particular historical value, and certainly no monetary value. What makes it holy...sacred...is the man for whose use it was set apart—the man to whom it once belonged, who had touched it and held it in his hands.

Do you see how we are surrounded by the sacred? God is speaking to us and touching us all the time, and we are most often too busy to even notice His attempts to get our attention.

When God enters a situation, it becomes sacred, and the lessons we learn become priceless. There are "Coke bottles" everywhere, amazing encounters with God—situations and conversations He has entered, sometimes almost in secret—and if we will train our ears and eyes to see Him there, all of life will become a prayer, a Bible study, an act of worship, or a great spiritual lesson on His love and grace.

When we see the sacred that surrounds us, we realize that our constant Companion and Friend walks with us every moment of every day, pointing out His reality in a world that is often too preoccupied with other things to notice the One they might encounter.

Now, every time I go into a store where they sell Coke in glass bottles, I buy one. Then I get in my car, open the cap, take a sip, and remember. And every single time it brings me back to one of the greatest days of my life, where 18 years of prayers were answered, and a great and holy God arranged an amazing encounter with one of His great and holy servants.

2

The Big Deal with Jesus

Salvation is found in no one else, for there is no other name under heaven given to men by which we must be saved.

—Acts 4:12

I HAVE BEEN ON SOME GREAT ADVENTURES and seen some incredibly interesting things. But until you've been on a cruise, you've never really lived. Preposterous? Well, bear with me for a moment.

First of all, there are people from nearly every nation on earth. A cruise ship is a bit like the United Nations on a boat. On a recent trip to Alaska, I met folks from the Philippines, Croatia, Serbia, Mexico, Russia, New Zealand, China, Japan, and that exotic country that is so mysterious to us Americans—Canada.

Second, I marvel at the sheer genius of the people who invented "the cruise." They charge you thousands of dollars to get on their ship, and once you get on board, they sail out to sea so you can't leave. But not to worry. Conveniently, they have thought of every possible scenario and have planned for all your basic needs, at a price equivalent to the gross national product of Australia. If you forgot your watch, they have an entire watch shop to offer you a variety of timepieces priced from $500 to $67,000. (Never mind that you're stuck on a cruise ship and can eat anytime you want, so you don't even need a watch.)

Third, there are massive quantities of alcohol available to the thirsty sailor, and the opportunities to purchase said spirits are promoted on the TV in your room, by your waiters at every meal, by servers at the movies and shows you attend, and in the newsletters they place in your room while you're out shopping for the watch you forgot.

I don't take any pleasure in watching people suffer the consequences of their decisions. But if I were to make an exception, it would be for watching drunken people on a cruise. You already have a giant boat going 25 knots over eight-foot waves into a 30-mile-per-hour headwind. Many of the people on the ship already have a hard time keeping their balance because of their age or their seasickness; now imagine those same people liquored up. The scene would be funny were it not so downright pitiful.

But perhaps the most awe-inspiring element of the cruise experience is the food. It's literally everywhere, all the time, in absurd quantities. All you can eat—and you can order anything at any time. On our trip to Alaska, I ate lobster tail, pheasant, and filet mignon all at one sitting. There were pizza bars, soup bars, dessert bars, ice-cream stations, an omelet station, a sandwich station, a fruit bar, and 24-hour room service. Eating is just one more thing to do while they have you locked in their seafaring vessel, and people do take advantage of it. My wife and I heard the cruise director tell us that for one eight-day journey, they had loaded 150 tons of food onto the ship.

∽

I enjoy observing people and places, and the cruise ship affords me great opportunity for this. I noticed something on our Alaskan cruise that struck me, at first, as a bit odd. Upon later reflection I realized it wasn't quite so weird after all.

The boat was decorated with all sorts of art and knick-knacks, some pretty classy and others just plain tacky. And it seemed that the same geniuses who thought up "the cruise" had also counted on the diversity of cultural backgrounds that would be represented on their voyages. They had therefore decorated the boat with that in mind.

In one of the bars, there was a mural of ancient Egypt, complete with a pharaoh, pyramids, ankhs, and religious symbols of the old Egyptian belief in the afterworld and the underworld. In the atrium there was a small wall dedicated to American patriotism, complete with the Statue of Liberty and a flowing American flag. Downstairs was a pub called Churchill's, decorated in old British style; pictures of the great prime minister hung on the walls, and old newspaper clippings from the time of World War II were framed above the tables. The spa was Asian in style, and all the descriptive literature boasted of an atmosphere where one could relieve tension and stress according to ancient Asian practices of meditation while considering the wisdom of great teachers like Confucius.

꩜

Midway through the trip, I was in the outdoor pool after a workout, trying to cool off. I was the only one out that day because it was freezing. I glanced around the steps and chairs and hot tubs and noticed right in the most prominent position, staring directly at me, was Buddha. A pedestal about three feet high was placed in the very middle of the pool area, and perched atop it was a statue of the founder of Buddhism.

So we stared at each other for a few seconds. Neither of us said anything. But I found it curious that so many symbols of the world, its religions and cultures, were incorporated into a luxury liner like this one.

I had just one question: Where was Jesus? There was no hint at all of Christian symbolism on the boat, even though Christianity is the world's largest religion.

Actually, though, I wasn't upset about it. I didn't feel slighted or overlooked, and I didn't think it was a conspiracy by socialists or liberals to eradicate Jesus from the public square. It actually felt correct, in a way.

So much of what happened on that ship was in direct contradiction to the example Jesus gives me. And though my wife and I relaxed and had a great time, how many people chose to stay intoxicated the entire trip, or waste their life savings at the casino every night? So it felt right that Jesus wasn't there in the form of some mindless statue. But there's more to it than that.

He stands above all others not just because of His good teachings or great ideas, but because of what they spring out of: His authority.

Jesus cannot be slapped unthinkingly onto a mural of cultural trinkets. I was glad I didn't see Jesus sandwiched between King Tut and Winston Churchill, because Jesus Christ is the Lord of the universe. All these other things were cheap icons—a flagrant attempt to incorporate some sort of diversity into the ship's atmosphere. Worse yet, maybe it wasn't really planned at all. Maybe someone just threw it all together for "artistic" scenery.

I actually would have felt sad if Jesus had been sitting on that perch by the pool instead of Buddha. What difference does it make to put Jesus on public display if He's not on the private throne of your heart? To merely say that Jesus is on a different level than all the other great teachers and leaders of history is like saying the *Titanic* took on a little bit of water.

Jesus is not on a different level. He's an altogether different person with an altogether different message. And this is the big deal with Him. He will not be one icon among others on the wall of cruise ship art. He will not look on passively as we ruin our lives by selfishly pursuing our own bliss.

He stands above all others not just because of His good teachings or great ideas, but because of what they spring out of: His authority. He refuses to glance, at our wasted lives and then turn away. Instead He commands us to repent of our selfish deeds. He refuses to capitulate to our freely chosen self-destruction and demands we cease serving ourselves and begin serving Him.

∽

How can I sum it up? What *is* the big deal with Jesus? Why does His name offend people? Why can a pastor pray in God's name at a presidential inauguration and never cause a stir, but when one prays in *Jesus'* name, the news networks talk about it for three weeks?

The reason is simple. Jesus commits the offense of claiming it all. He wants it all. He demands you and me and the world, all our allegiance and all our love. He doesn't want to be *first* on our list—He wants to *be* the list. He won't settle for being equal with all other faiths and founders, or even a notch or two above. He claims authority by His death and resurrection over the entire universe and its inhabitants. This world is His. Jesus is Lord over gravity and air. He wins.

He is a big deal because He is God, and nobody else is. Any other claims to that position are wrong. And so, giving Jesus a place among all the other icons on a cruise ship would be a stupid joke—especially when He made the ocean the ship floats upon.

3

Braces at 34

It was good for me to be afflicted so that
I might learn your decrees.

—Psalm 119:71

I can remember being surrounded by old people all my life. This meant I also heard details—too many details—about getting old and the aches, pains, and headaches that come with age. Some of my older relatives would talk about health "issues" that to us were completely taboo, but to them seemed absolutely normal.

For that reason I've always lived with a sense of impending doom that one day I would be old, my entire body would hurt all day and night, I would never eat or sleep normally again, and I would pine for the lost days of my youth. In a way, however, I'm actually thankful that old age can't sneak up on me like it does on other people. I was warned.

Sure enough, many people, including my own father, were amazingly accurate about what my mid-thirties were going to be like. I almost dreaded that decade more than my 60s or 70s because of the mountain of bad news I was given. I was told my vision would start to blur; my hearing would diminish (usually in one ear first, then the other); my joints would begin to ache, especially my knees (from all the years of sports and running); and my energy level would suddenly plummet.

I would start going to bed at 9 p.m., and I would snore—loudly. I would also begin waking up before 6 a.m., unable to sleep any longer because of the pain in my neck and hips. My music tastes would change from hard rock to easy listening, even a little jazz. The list went on and on—and so far, most of it has come true or is in the process.

What kind of encounter with God can be found in all of this? Well, remember, His truth can be found if we know where to look for it. All truth is, after all, His truth, and the echoes and reflections of His gospel and work of redemption swirl around us every single day. We just seldom sit still long enough, or reflect deeply enough, to see.

∽

I had another of those amazing encounters at age 34. I had it when the dentist said some terrifying words to me as I sat motionless in his chair. What had been a haven of safety and predictability my entire life now became a place of panic as the frightening news broke in without any warning:

"Clayton, you are going to need braces."

These words, delivered so matter-of-factly, could just as well have been a report of an impending invasion of the U.S. by the Royal Canadian Mounted Police. It was so clearly absurd that I figured he couldn't possibly be serious.

"What? Like, the ones that go on my teeth? There's no way I am going to do that." I began to recite to my dentist all the reasons I couldn't possibly consider his suggestion:

1. I couldn't afford it. No way, nohow, was I going to pay $6400 for braces.
2. I couldn't bear the pain. Those things hurt, badly, and were constantly aggravating.

3. I speak to over 300,000 people a year, and I wasn't about to do it with a piece of spinach stuck between shards of metal glued to my incisors.
4. With my busy schedule, I didn't have the time to go to an orthodontist once a month—or sit with sixth-graders and their parents in the waiting room.
5. I was unwilling to give up gum, ice, chips, or nuts—especially almonds, which are rich in protein and enzymes that protect from heart disease. If I had to stop eating almonds, I would die of a heart attack—all because of the braces.
6. To be totally honest, I was simply embarrassed by the idea. I mean, I'm all about keeping it real with the kids, but good night! Getting braces so I could relate to the teenagers I was preaching to was going a little overboard!

My dentist responded calmly, assuring me I indeed had the right to opt out of braces. But the consequences would be severe. He had his own list of reasons, reasons why I *had* to get braces.

1. My teeth looked straight to the naked eye, but actually they were off by four nanometers.
2. As a public communicator it would be in my professional interest to look attractive on stage, especially as technology changed and my face was being plastered on big screens more often when I spoke.
3. Crooked teeth could be a distraction to my audiences, so it would be in my best interest spiritually to stop the possible downward spiral of my preaching ministry.
4. As I aged, my teeth would get weaker and separate more, allowing food particles to lodge in the small crevices. The sugar deposits in those hard-to-reach places would cause decay, eventually resulting in the loss of my own, rotten teeth and the advent of fake choppers.
5. The most obvious reason, however, was my "exploded

> canine." This sounds like a cruel animal trick at a magic show, but actually it's a technical term. One of my teeth had emerged high in the gum of my upper left jaw. At 34 I still had a baby canine tooth, and the permanent tooth had "exploded" above the baby tooth, never pushing it out. The baby tooth would eventually die, the "exploded canine" would stay too high and fuse to the jawbone, and I would be left with an unsightly gap. All my upper teeth would shift to fill in the gap, messing up my bite and eroding the enamel, which would expose every tooth in my mouth to all sorts of evil. (Then, through a series of related events, global warming would speed up, the polar ice caps would melt, and a giant meteor would strike the planet. America would revert to being a British colony, and VCRs would replace all modern imaging technology.)

The dentist made a compelling case. I thought about it, prayed about it, and then decided to do the wisest thing I can do in situations of such great importance. I consulted my wife.

This time it was a gargantuan mistake. She laughed, giggled, and howled when she learned I would be forced to go through painful and humiliating torture for 18 months.

I know she loves me, but she also enjoys laughing at me—which I don't mind if I've said or done something clever or humorous. But this was different.

Once she got over enjoying herself at my expense, she explained she had already suffered through braces as a teenager, and she said it was "easy" once you got used to it. She promised to help me through the hard days. She told me about wax and gargling with salt water, what to do when you have a sore on your gums, and how to get food out of your braces with tongue gymnastics—without ever opening your mouth or using sharp objects. Though she tried to sound encouraging, she kept flashing a gleeful grin. I figured this meant she would secretly enjoy watching me endure a painful adolescent experience in my mid-thirties.

Of course, I opted for the braces. What else could I do? The fate of the world, not to mention the cosmos, depended on it. And I've hated *every single second* with them. They hurt. They ache. They stick. They cut. They scrape. They leave indentations on the inside of my mouth, and when I have to get them tightened or have the chain replaced, for days I can't chew food without feeling like the roots of every tooth are being driven through my skull into my brain. Pain medicine is useless. I just eat soup and drink milkshakes.

Can anything so painful and disruptive actually be helpful? Because if there's no upside, an individual would have to be clinically insane to endure this.

The Holy Spirit has been rather vocal throughout my braces phase. He has revealed that there's indeed an upside, a benefit, to the inconvenience. He has shown me on numerous occasions the similarities between the pain I've endured at the hands of my orthodontist and the pain I've endured at the hands of God. Both mean me no harm, but rather wish me to be better off in the long run. But in order for me to be in a better, healthier state in the future, some drastic measures have to be taken in the present to ensure the result. What is the end result with braces? Straight, healthy teeth. And to get there, pain must be inflicted. Measures taken. Money paid. Metal and wire added. X-rays done and people's hands stuck in your mouth. Brushing after every meal. All for one purpose, one eventual goal: straight, healthy teeth.

> In order for God to bend me, shape me, and turn me into a man who resembles His Son, He has to apply some pressure. And pressure hurts.

What is the end result of the Christian life? Simply put, it's to know God through Jesus Christ and to be transformed into His image. To be made right, and pure, and holy. To be...made straight?

In order for God to bend me, shape me, and turn me into a man who resembles His Son, He has to apply some pressure. And pressure hurts. It's impossible to correct crooked teeth without pain, and it's equally impossible for God to remake us into the image of Jesus without hurting us.

Just as teeth have to be coerced into cooperation against their crooked will, my own disposition has to be coerced and forced, pushed and pulled, against my own stubborn will.

This cannot be done gently, though it must be done slowly. God employs every tool and implement to accomplish His purpose in me, no matter how much I may hate it, beg for mercy, or implore Him to stop. He can see the end result, and it's the end result He has in mind, because that is what we'll live with forever—and ultimately, that is what matters most.

4

For Sale

The man who received the one talent came. "Master," he said, "I knew that you are a hard man, harvesting where you have not sown and gathering where you have not scattered seed. So I was afraid and went out and hid your talent in the ground. See, here is what belongs to you." His master replied, "You wicked, lazy servant!"

—Matthew 25:24-26

My college days were some of the best years of my life. As a matter of fact, I loved my four years at the university so much that I would gladly go back and repeat them. (I know not everyone can say that.)

One thing that made my university experience so positive and fulfilling was the spiritual nature of the entire time. I surrounded myself with strong believers who shared common goals and convictions, and I had some professors who helped mold me into a minister who loved the gospel and the Scripture. One such professor, Dr. Cullinan, was loved and respected by students and faculty for her personal care and concern for each student as well as her intellect. She was my academic advisor and a personal mentor as well.

My favorite class with her was "American Religious Groups."

This was essentially a study on cults, fringe "Christian" churches, and unorthodox groups with strange beliefs, as well as the different Christian denominations among Protestants. Part of our class assignment required us to visit the worship services of four of these groups. One of the groups I chose was the Seventh-Day Adventists.

∽

I visited a Seventh-Day Adventist church on a Saturday because that is the day they worship, believing they are required to gather corporately on the Jewish Sabbath in accordance with Old Testament tradition. I found the service itself strange and boring because I was accustomed to a more lively corporate worship experience, and because it contained so much of their strange theology and traditions, with which I was absolutely unfamiliar. But since they met on Saturdays, they used the sanctuary of an Associate Reformed Presbyterian (ARP) church in Woodruff, a small town just seven miles from where I grew up.

That Saturday, I found myself more interested in the architecture of the sanctuary than the message or the music. The building was very old, both on the inside and outside. It smelled old—archaic and full of history. I'd driven past the place literally hundreds of times over the years and had always been impressed by the giant oak trees outside and the humongous graveyard on the south side. The gravestones interested me—many were Gothic in appearance and looked European in style.

The building was located in a historic part of Woodruff. Several antebellum mansions stood on the same street, just a stone's throw away. I arrived a half hour early that cool autumn morning and strolled through the church grounds, looking at the dates and names on the gravestones. Some of them dated back to the early 1700s. History has always been my favorite subject, so as I indicated, I was more interested in the past of that church than in taking notes on the Seventh-Day Adventist worship experience.

I was able to speak with a custodian that day, and he told me that the ARP Church of Woodruff was one of the oldest congregations in upstate South Carolina. It had been vibrant for hundreds of years, including among its members doctors, attorneys, businessmen, and farmers who held great influence in their town. The church trained and sent dozens of young men into ministry. Many of them attended seminary about an hour away at Erskine College, the only ARP seminary in America. Their summer revivals would last for weeks at a time, and many new converts to faith were welcomed.

He lamented that the ARP congregation now consisted of a handful of elderly people in their seventies and eighties. Once they all died, he said, the church would close the doors. They were happy to rent the building to the Seventh-Day Adventists to make a little extra money to pay the ARP pastor.

∽

That conversation took place in 1994. Thirteen years later, my wife and I and our two boys were heading back to my parents' house for a holiday visit; and like I'd done for years, I turned onto Highway 101 in Woodruff. As I passed the old ARP church on my right, I noticed a huge sign in the front:

FOR SALE

Somehow, that made me very sad. I recalled the Saturday I'd walked the graveyard and read the tombstones, admiring the unfamiliar architecture and the musty smell of the old sanctuary. I imagined once more what those old revival services must have been like: People coming from all around in wagons, on horses, or on foot, with the farmers still in their overalls fresh from the cotton fields, and the local bankers and businessmen dressed in their fine tweed suits and fedora hats. I remembered the conversation with the custodian, who had recalled the glory days and predicted the eventual demise of a once-mighty church. His prediction had come true.

And I pondered this question: For the church, is there anything worse than death? I thought about that for several days before I found the answer.

Yes, there is something worse than death: irrelevance. The church building was for sale not because the few remaining members had died, but because the congregation itself had been dead for decades. It had died when it had become irrelevant to the people and the needs of the community it existed to serve. It died when the mission of the gospel became less important than their mission of holding on until death took place.

Reading the tombstones of our ancestors in the faith may inspire faithfulness in us, but it doesn't translate into engaging our communities with the gospel by serving them and showing them the love of Christ.

Relevance seems to be one of the buzzwords of the contemporary, emerging church of our day. But I don't use the word lightly, because I feel it carries such importance with it. Though I don't think the church exists only to meet the needs of people, I also believe that if the church ignores outreach, missions, evangelism, and service to those on the outside who need the gospel, we quickly slide into selfish isolation where our only concern is us—what we need, what we want...preserving the past and protecting our turf. This is exactly what happened to the ARP church, and it's exactly what is happening to thousands of churches all over our country.

I'm truly saddened that a once-great church no longer exists in that community. It's sad that a great legacy of faithfulness and ministry died out with the few remaining members. Now all that remains is a dilapidated though historic brick building surrounded by an old graveyard filled with bones of dead men...who could tell really inspiring stories of the good old days.

∽

There's another part of me, however, that rejoices in all of this. When the people of God stop caring about the world they are called to love and serve, they turn inward, and as a result they actually undermine the mission of the church by showing the world that they are selfish and irrelevant. We do more damage than good when we get to that place, and the best thing that can happen is for the end to come quickly. As when we pray for a dying loved one to pass away soon without too much suffering, the most merciful thing we can wish for a dead and irrelevant church is that it go quickly before inflicting too much damage on the world outside.

Of course, it's best if a church like this turns around in repentance and brokenness, seeking God's forgiveness and a new vision for reaching their community with the gospel. This is the ideal. But when the church is unwilling to embrace God's mission, then let's bring on the inevitable and put out the "for sale" sign.

Nostalgia for the good old days will never make any difference for the kingdom of God today. Memories of great revival meetings in the past bring no one into God's grace today. And reading the tombstones of our ancestors in the faith may inspire faithfulness in us, but it doesn't translate into engaging our communities with the gospel by serving them and showing them the love of Christ.

The good old days were certainly great. But one thing's for sure: They are gone and never coming back. Instead of holding the fort until we are all dead, let's move forward and possess the land.

5

The Fine Art of Forgiveness

Be kind and compassionate to one another, forgiving each other, just as in Christ God forgave you.

—Ephesians 4:32

THERE I WAS ON ANOTHER AIRPLANE. (Sometimes I think the airlines should give me a volume discount; other times I wonder if they should bill me for rent.) After two decades of flying, you'd think I would remember by now that an encounter with God awaits me in the experience. In the purgatory of Atlanta-Hartsfield International or aboard the puddle jumper from Memphis to Tupelo, He sends me some of the strangest and most interesting people.

And in their faces and our conversations, I sense divine lessons. One of these I'm still trying to implement in my own life—that to live for Christ means to die to self—to my personal agendas and selfish ambitions. Amazingly, on one particular day I would meet two people who would teach me what it meant to die to my need for vengeance and justice.

I love history, especially the era of the Second Great War (World

War II, that is). As I get older, there are fewer and fewer veterans of that great, history-defining conflict with which to share conversation. On the rare occasion that I do meet a veteran of that war, I hang on his every word. This is especially so now because my grandfather (a navy man who served in the South Pacific) is no longer alive to reluctantly answer the questions I dared ask him about his experience.

∞

Back to the airplane. I was in the aisle seat next to a cute and obviously "foreign" older married couple. (The word *foreign* has fallen on hard times in this soft day. I use it here to emphasize that this couple stood out, in a positive and nonoffensive way, as an interesting and cutely odd sort of duo, one I desired to meet.)

They looked to be in their eighties and clearly cared for each other deeply. They embodied an honor and dignity of not only another country, but another age—that of people who had endured a hard life with aplomb and grace, and wore the experience in the lines on their faces and the creases around their deep, dark eyes.

The two were indeed married, and had been for over 60 years. Vito, the husband, had left home before he turned 20 to serve Mussolini in the Italian army, leaving his young bride behind. In his striking accent and syncopated English, he recalled for me the horrors and fears of serving a cause he believed in his heart was evil and unjust...and how he wanted so badly to run away, to take his wife to a place with no war, no Hitler or Hirohito, and start over. But he followed orders and prayed at night that God would forgive him for the things he did and saw in battle. Then everything changed.

He was in a company of Italian soldiers who were captured by the Russians. According to Vito, the Russians were cut from the same evil cloth as the Germans, but in bigger pieces. As a prisoner of war, he was gagged, tied, and dragged from place to place to place. He had no idea from one day to the next what country he was in, but he was certain when the harsh cold caused frostbite in his toes and fingers that he must have been far away from any part of Western Europe.

Daily he was beaten and cursed. All the prisoners were subjected to inhuman conditions, much of it the inevitable result of prison-camp life: roaches, rats, lice, darkness, diarrhea. Vito felt like God was punishing him for fighting for Mussolini and decided he deserved it. He resolved to die there and never again see his wife or set foot on the rich soil of his homeland where the Caesars had walked.

Then he had a change of heart—or mind, or courage, or probably all three. Vito got, for lack of a better term, a second wind. Despite the consequences, he planned an escape attempt. He didn't tell me how he escaped (though I would have loved to hear the details), but somehow, against all odds, he got out undetected and made his way through the vast Russian wilderness. He hitched rides in railcars. He slept in ditches and barns. In one small village, in the darkness of a stranger's barn, he killed and ate a chicken, then drank the milk he got from a cow.

His voice turned especially tender when he spoke of the Russian peasants who offered him lodging with nothing more than a nod and a smile, unable to communicate in words with an Italian POW. I wondered how many Russian families that offered him haven had sacrificed their own husbands and children in the war. Perhaps they had even battled against Vito in some nameless town, and here he was, sitting at their table eating bread from their hearth.

He wandered for nearly two years, crossing borders with the help (I assume) of other soldiers, merchants, farmers, villagers, and vagabonds. Figuring that his wife had given him up for dead, he pressed on in the hope that she would not have remarried before he made it home, but holding no ill will toward her if she had. People along the way fed him and gave him clothing—including shoes to replace the many pairs he wore out on the journey from the steppes of Russia to his devastated Italian homeland, laid waste by demonic ideologies and a madman filled with lust for blood and power.

The long-awaited day finally arrived: the day when he rounded the corner, gazed upon his home, still intact, and found his wife in the yard hanging clothes on the line. At first his heart sank when he saw her. What if she no longer loved him? What if there was a new husband inside their old home?

Without a word, as if she sensed him there, she turned and caught his gaze. Their eyes met, and a deep sadness filled her face when she realized the man she looked upon was gaunt and thin from unspeakable experiences she had hoped she would never hear of, but longed to know. She ran into his arms; he hugged her tight and kissed her tenderly, and as the long journey home was completed, a longer journey was just beginning—the journey toward forgiveness.

∞

Vito had to learn to live again. Years of an existence worse than an animal's and of being treated as a nonhuman had all but murdered his hope in humanity. But the undeserved kindness shown to him by strangers—enemy strangers in enemy territory—had softened a heart that had grown hard and tough. Two years of memories were laid one upon the other in his mind—hundreds of difficult days and nights he had traversed rivers and woods, receiving kindness from the very people he had waged war on. Never mind that it was against his will. Russians were considered sadistic and merciless, and he had felt the sting of their punishments. But lodged in his soul were other portraits of Russians: kindness, generosity, sacrifice, and forgiveness.

Slowly he began to tell me how the good done to him by the poor, rural Russian farmers started to eat away at the hatred for the brutal men in the Siberian POW camp and the heartless deeds done to him. Love had won. Evil had done its best to crush Vito, but good had triumphed. He came to terms with the evil that lies within the human capacity to hurt, and he had concluded that the good was stronger than the bad.

With tears in his eyes, he repeated over and over again the phrase,

"I forgave them, I forgave them all!" His wife clung to his hand, smiling and offering her silent support—thankful, I'm sure, that God had brought her husband back to her and that they had lived their lives together after she feared he was forever gone.

I asked Vito how long it had taken him to forgive the guards who tortured him. His reply was simple: "Oh, I am still forgiving them. When I decided to forgive them for hurting me, it did not end there; it only began. Every day I am tempted to hate them again, but every day I choose to forgive them instead of hating them. I will be forgiving them until I die."

☙

How often do we assume that if we could just get to a place of being willing to let an offense go, we would be free from it, never to pick it up again? But true forgiveness not only starts the process—it sticks with it. The human heart is not designed to forget, and we almost never forget wrongs done to us.

As soon as we decide to forgive a person, right away the thought comes to us that they don't deserve it—they aren't sorry, they would do it again, they have no idea how they wounded us—and then we decide that we aren't so sure we meant what we said. But the kind of forgiveness given to us by God in Jesus Christ is the benchmark. Forgiveness is not to be extended on the basis of earned merit, humble repentance, sufficient restitution, or contrite apologies. Forgiveness is to be offered simply because it's the right thing to do. It holds the moral high ground, offering the promise of peace to the offended forgiver as well as the guilty offender—if they choose to give and receive it with no strings attached.

In Christ not only do resentment and unforgiveness die, the right to be offended dies. The right to be angry dies. The need to be proven right, or get even, dies.

In Christ all our wrong deeds, all causes of bitterness, die. In Christ not only do resentment and unforgiveness die, the right to be offended dies. The right to be angry dies. The need to be proven right, or get even, dies.

When we decide, like the disciple Thomas, to go with Christ so we may die with Him, a slow and certain death begins—the death of all inside us that refuses to offer to others the forgiveness granted to us by Jesus.

6

Greener Grass

Why be captivated, my son, by an adulteress? Why embrace the bosom of another man's wife? For a man's ways are in full view of the Lord, and he examines all his paths.

—Proverbs 5:20-21

SINCE I BEGAN THIS CHRISTIAN JOURNEY over 20 years ago, I've slowly noticed how God makes His presence evident to me in clear and unmistakable ways, often when I least expect it or when I'm looking in the opposite direction.

In college and seminary, I was challenged to hone the discipline of "theological reflection." In this discipline I simply train my eyes, my ears, my head, and my heart to notice, in the everyday occurrences and conversations of my life, threads of God's reality and the gospel. And like the body is trained to run long distances in a marathon, my heart and my mind have become, over the years, trained to look for these amazing glimpses of God.

Anyone who has talked to me for more than five minutes (or has read chapter 1 in this book) knows how much I love and admire Billy

Graham—and his Coke bottle. One thing I've learned from observing his ministry is that it pays off in the long run to place a high value on personal integrity. Now in his nineties, he has maintained the highest standard ever seen in a prominent public figure.

By the grace of God, and using him as an example, I've tried to implement many of the moral defenses and spiritual precautions that have safeguarded him. But there's another reason I'm so very serious about living out personal integrity, particularly in the area of relationship with the opposite sex.

To put it bluntly, I'm paralyzed with horror at the number of men who have fallen into sexual sin over the past two decades—men I've known personally, who I've preached for, who I've broken bread with and shared fellowship with. I could fill the pages of another book with the gut-wrenching conversations I've had with brothers before, during, and after they were seduced, or walked willingly and lustfully into an adulterous relationship.

I still feel sick when I think about a confrontation with a young man in ministry who was sleeping with a 19-year-old he met on a mission trip. He had left his wife and two children and was hiding out with a friend to avoid all his brothers in Christ. We eventually found him and gave him an ultimatum. The look of death came across his face when he turned to me and said, "I am willing to lose everything for this girl because I love her, and I will not apologize or go back home."

The girl eventually left him, and he's serving time in prison now for evading law enforcement and failing to pay child support. There's always a day of reckoning.

∽

I was on my way home recently when my cell phone rang. (I hate talking on the phone in the car, but I hate even more catching up on calls at home when I could be spending time with my wife and boys.) So I answered. And within a few minutes, I regretted that decision.

On the other line was a good friend, one I had known for nearly two decades. And he didn't call to share good news. He called to tell me that a colleague in ministry, whom we both knew, had just been caught in adultery. This man had been living a double life; while his popularity was growing as a speaker and preacher nationwide, he had for many years been having a secret affair with a young woman.

When his sin was uncovered, it naturally devastated all those involved. He lost his church; his wife left him, heartbroken and bitter; his kids were disillusioned; his ministry was destroyed. It was a soul-sucking conversation to have, and it seems like I have them more often these days. I was in a state of shock as I drove home, phone in hand, praying it would never happen to me.

෴

To get to our house, I need to pass miles of soybean fields and pastures, old farmhouses, cows, horses, and the occasional wild deer or turkey. So driving past all this, I was on the phone listening to the gut-wrenching story of another man of God who'd stepped out of bounds, when I saw something I'd seen dozens of times before. But not like this.

It was a horse eating grass. Nothing special about that—except that, because of the news I'd just heard, I was keenly aware of the striking picture presented by this common sight.

> No matter how enticing and delicious sin may pretend to be, it never satisfies our souls. It just keeps lying to us, telling us we need more of it to be happy.

This horse had his head stuck between the strands of a barbed wire fence and was stretching the wire to the point of breaking it. He had plenty of green grass *inside* the fence. It was no different from what he was feasting on through the barbed wire. Same grass, different location. And the old phrase came to mind: "The grass is always greener on the other side."

Where that phrase had come from immediately struck home, as did the striking similarity between that horse and the pastor who had just had a moral failure. Both had what they needed on their side of the fence. Both decided to stretch the boundaries a bit. And that pastor had paid a severe price for a momentary pleasure that was now completely gone.

How utterly dumb it was of my ministry colleague to venture outside the boundaries and safety of marriage and actually believe it would be better than what he already had! Just like that dumb horse straining and pushing through the pain of sharp metal barbs poking his skin, this man's animal desire to have something off-limits had taken over. I actually pulled off the road to watch this horse eat while thinking about the agony brought on a family and a church community because one man could not be satisfied with his own wife.

∽

No matter how enticing and delicious sin may pretend to be, it never satisfies our souls. It just keeps lying to us, telling us we need more of it to be happy. But we can never get enough. Using sin to satisfy your soul is eating salt when you're dying of thirst. The more we sin, the more desperately we need Jesus to forgive us and truly satisfy our longings. The grass is never greener on the other side. *Never.*

That image is burned into my mind now. I pass that same horse in that same pasture every day, and I make a conscious effort to pray every single time for protection and purity. I ask the Lord to guard me from the things that would beckon and entice me to push through the fence. And I recall that, just as the fence was put there to keep the horse from wandering into the road and getting hit by a truck, God gives us commandments and boundaries for our protection, not our punishment. As C.S. Lewis wrote, if children are playing on the edge of a cliff, are they happier when they are free from restraint, or are they happier when they are playing behind the safety and security of a fence, one that was put there for their good? We enjoy life when we stay in the security of God's boundaries.

It could happen to me. And you. Only by God's grace have we not disqualified ourselves with some stupid lust or demonic desire. There's a subtle evil that lives in each of us, a worldly wanderlust that always wants what we can't, or shouldn't, have.

And I saw myself in that horse, sticking my neck out, straining hard, and enduring pain for something that would never satisfy even for a single moment.

I prayed that God would restore a fallen brother, mend a broken marriage, and heal bitter children who were suffering the effects of the sin of their father.

And I prayed for myself, and all my brothers and sisters, that we would not be tricked by the false promise of greener grass...but that we would simply find deep joy in what we already have in one another, in the Word of God, and ultimately in knowing Christ Jesus, our Lord.

7

Our Advantage over Ants

Go to the ant, you sluggard; consider its ways and be wise!

—Proverbs 6:6

Be self-controlled and alert. Your enemy the devil prowls around like a roaring lion looking for someone to devour.

—1 Peter 5:8

All my life I was taught that Christians weren't allowed to hate anyone. I understood this easily enough. Jesus loved people, we loved Jesus, and so we needed to love people, not hate them. But it took me a few years to come to grips with the other things I naturally hated. Would you like to know some of the things I naturally hate? Okay, here goes!

1. *Math:* With obligatory apologies to all the math teachers who are picking up a calculus book to hurl at me, my mind just wasn't cut out for this stuff. The funny thing is, when it comes to money, numbers seem to flow naturally for me. I've never balanced my checkbook, since I always

know in my head exactly how much I have in the bank. But it's all the addition, division, and symbols that make me want to jump off a cliff.

2. *Golf:* Egads! What do people see in this sport? Maybe when I turn 40 I'll discover it. But until then, as long as I can spend my time doing more exciting things like trimming my fingernails or spreading mulch, I will hold off on golf.
3. *Spiders:* I have an unreasonable fear of any arachnid other than a daddy longlegs, and I usually squeal like a girl until my wife or one of my little boys comes to kill a spider that's got me backed up against a wall. In college I punched one of my closest friends square in the jaw because he chased me into the bathroom with a dead brown recluse. (They all thought it was funny, but who's laughing now?)

I never dreamed I would say anything like this, but God actually taught me something using a spider. Yep—I had an amazing encounter with Him, and an arachnid was involved.

∞

Occasionally we reward our boys with a trip to Chick-fil-A, a restaurant that's everywhere in the South. (Their mom and dad love it too.) I can read a free copy of the newspaper while my boys throw other kids off the playground equipment. Their coffee is pretty good, and their Polynesian sauce could be sold in bottles and poured over everything from steak to pound cake. To top it off, I just *love* it when they hand you your order and, in response to your "Thank you," they reply, "My pleasure!" Chick-fil-A has returned manners and kindness to the fast-food industry.

We were heading home one afternoon, and for some reason we had missed lunch by an hour. My boys were consuming the upholstery and were certain to start cannibalizing each other next. I decided to spend the cash and get them some nuggets at Chick-fil-A while treating myself to a vanilla milkshake.

We approached the window to pay for our order, and a gruesome sight caught my eye. Underneath the small counter at the window was an intricate spider web; trapped in the web was a very big ant. It had wings, so it must have been a flying ant (I've mastered the art of deductive reasoning).

As the ant spun and struggled, the sticky web wrapped around its wings. The more control it lost, the more panicked it became. It began losing steam fast. After jerking and rolling, it was reduced to a steady twitch of its legs. Finally, exhausted from the futile frenzy, it just quit moving.

I began to see all the similarities between the spider catching the ant and our own lives as we succumb to the well-thought-out plans and schemes of Satan himself!

I knew what was coming. Something inside me told me to turn away, but I had to look. Triumphantly, a brown spider emerged from its dark and diabolical lair, where it had perched hungrily, waiting for the ant to expend its energy. The sinister creature could then saunter toward its powerless prey.

I was filled with horror and rage. I'd always hated these crafty creatures, and now I knew why. The spider, only half the size of the ant, was in no hurry to dine—it knew its prey was safe and sound in its grasp. It had done this before—it had seen its web-building abilities capture more than one tasty meal. It mounted the writhing body and bit the ant on the head, injecting (I assumed) some potent poison to kill it. I wondered how cruelly long the spider would wait before digging in.

Suddenly I heard my sons yelling from the backseat. "Daddy, pay attention! The woman is talking to you! She's trying to give you our lunch. We want our food!" (The girl at the drive-through window had been trying to hand me a bag of waffle fries, but I'd seemed so engrossed in thought that she'd been afraid to startle me.)

I apologized, took our food, and drove home, disgusted at what I'd witnessed, and more convinced than ever that one day God would rid our world of spiders so that all life could exist in harmony and peace. I felt soiled by having watched such a vile villain, the nemesis of my childhood nightmares, inflict its heinous cruelty. I had lost my appetite.

∞

Sitting at the red light not a minute later, it hit me. Watching that well-planned attack showed me how much spiders are like the devil. In a rush of revelation, I began to see all the similarities between the spider catching the ant and our own lives as we succumb to the well-thought-out plans and schemes of Satan himself! I grabbed a napkin out of the waffle fries bag and began to jot down thoughts so I wouldn't forget them.

Satan is wise and crafty. He's also experienced. It's said that Socrates once told his students, "Youth and energy are no match for age and cunning." Our enemy, the devil, has been laying traps for God's children since the day he slithered into Eden on the belly of a snake. He's patient and willing to wait. And as he spins whatever web he believes will finally capture us, he recalls every other man or woman he ever caught in the same kind of trap. But he has more than one kind of web. He can customize.

I also thought it was strange that the spider was much smaller than the ant it captured. In a fair fight on level ground, the spider was no match for the giant ant. So the spider had to cheat—leverage its advantage of surprise and rely on brains, not brawn. The same is true for us. Satan is a defeated enemy because of the death and resurrection of Jesus on the cross. He knows he cannot win face-to-face, so he never announces his schemes or broadcasts his plans. He hides and waits. He taunts us and tricks us. He stays invisible just long enough for us to forget how real and dangerous he is, and once we have let our guard down, he pounces. Caught unaware, we are stuck before we know it, oftentimes without a chance to fight back.

Sin and temptation are like the web that lures us. It could be the thought of a secret rendezvous with an old girlfriend, or a secret late-night visit to a Web site. It could be a little money stuck in your pocket from the cash register at work, or a "little white lie" on your tax form. Either way, the web is sticky and strong, and it won't let go.

And once temptation has won and sin is committed, we feel guilty, condemned, shamed, and regretful. This is when the devil crawls out of his hole. He gloats over his apparent victory. He savors his own clever ability to trick and trap another child of God.

Am I going too far with this analogy? I don't think so, especially since Peter went so far as to refer to the devil as a roaring lion. My spider analogy is tame compared to that.

So are we all just doomed? Is it just a matter of time before we crawl into temptation, get stuck in a death trap, and wind up ruined? Is this our inevitable fate? Hardly.

We have an advantage over ants. And I reflected on this as I drove my boys home while they sucked down nuggets drowned in Polynesian sauce.

Ants, though they're mentioned in the Old Testament as examples of hard work, aren't intellectually advanced like humans. Our advantage lies in our ability to preempt pitfalls and problems. We observe life. We watch what happens when we make certain decisions, and (hopefully) we learn from mistakes and missteps. We then avoid certain behaviors and choices that place us in precarious situations, or that cause us great loss and regret. Think of Albert Einstein's definition of insanity: repeating the same behavior and expecting a different result.

But for a Christian, our advantage over ants goes beyond good old common sense. God has also warned us throughout Scripture about the schemes and plans of the evil one. We are told to avoid them, to watch out for them, to not be surprised by them. Sometimes we are told to fight against them, but other times to run away. In other words, we have God on our side, speaking words of warning and wisdom. He genuinely loves us and doesn't want us destroyed.

God is our advantage over ants and all other insects and animals. He doesn't want us to be humans who run headlong into stupidity and ruin. He warns us in the Bible. He warns us through our friends and fellow believers. He also warns us through the Holy Spirit, who lives in our hearts and guides us into truth and wisdom.

The best-case scenario for the ant is to avoid the sticky web altogether. Once caught, it's curtains. The same advice applies to me. If I see what alcohol consumption has done to numerous friends and colleagues, not to mention family members, then why not just avoid it completely? When I look at the lives of people who live for the weekend, the clubs, or the bars, hooking up with a stranger for a tryst, and I realize they're depressed and never keep a job for more than a few months, I make a mental note. When I read about successful businessmen who lose their families because of addictions to pornography, gambling, or strip clubs, why would I ever even entertain the idea of walking close to that web?

ꟹ

So what happens if we blow it? We get too close to the edge and wind up stuck, panicked, and helpless? Well, the good news is, we have a God who is quick to forgive and is also able to help get us out of tight spots. We aren't doomed if we sin. We do it all the time, after all. And He's there to convict us and call us to repentance. He does, however, want more than just a big "thank you" when He forgives us. He wants us to change our behavior, to practice wisdom in our living and choosing.

And make no mistake—just because He grants us grace and forgiveness is no guarantee that we'll escape the consequences of our sin. We may still have to pay a high price in this life for the offense. God seldom takes away the immediate consequences of our actions, but instead allows the natural process to play out, in essence teaching us sacred lessons as we suffer the results of the poor choices we made in rebellion against Him.

So now I have this mental image seared into my mind of a giant ant being annihilated by a tiny spider. And when temptations arise in my life to lust, or throw a fit of rage, or linger on an evil or vindictive thought, I remember that dumb ant walking right into a trap, and I tell myself that I'm smarter than ants. I have an advantage over them. And by God's grace, I move on, free of the clutches of evil, to enjoy the freedom of the life Christ has given me.

So, do I now look forward to encounters with spiders? Not by a long shot. But if God can meet me through a gruesome incident with a spider, then He can indeed meet me anywhere and anytime.

8

Believing Our Beliefs

Do not merely listen to the word, and so deceive yourselves. Do what it says.

—James 1:22

It's easy to give someone a list of our "beliefs" about all sorts of issues. We may know immediately where we stand on abortion, gay marriage, prayer in schools, or the authority of Scripture. I often hear people, when listing off their official beliefs, defer to their denomination. "Well, we're Methodist, so we don't see drinking alcohol as a sin." Or, "We're Baptist, and we think it's God's will that every Sunday church service be followed by a covered dish lunch that includes fried chicken and sweet tea." (Only true Baptists will understand that reference—and if they are really Baptist, they'll say, *"Amen!"*)

But do we really believe our beliefs? Are they genuine to our soul? Have we thought through why they made our list? If really challenged, could we defend why we believe our set of strongly held beliefs to be true? I'm afraid much of what passes for genuine belief is just passed-down faith—the hand-me-downs of ancestors or parents.

There's a very big and diverse world outside the walls of the church. Most people who live in that world think we're a bit weird. Sure, they may respect our right to believe what we choose—you know, the whole freedom of religion thing and the First Amendment, and so on—but those who aren't following Jesus can tell if we really believe our beliefs. They can sniff out a fake a mile away, and they have much better discernment than some Christians.

What would happen if Christians really believed all that we say we know, trust, and stand for? What would it be like if all the skeptics saw our "beliefs" in action, rather than just hearing them in sound bites on the evening news?

∞

I can give you at least one example, one I witnessed in a major airport. It was February 2001; I was on the last international trip I would make before September 11. We had been in India for several weeks, serving local churches, participating in a Bible-college graduation, and attending the wedding of two great friends, one Indian and one American. On our way home, during a layover in Bombay (now called Mumbai), we quickly realized that this was also the layover spot for hundreds of hippies, beatniks, potheads, wanderers, and full-time tourist-travelers. They had all been to the beaches of Goa, a place with a magnetic pull for countless young European souls looking for cheap drugs, easy sex, and endless sunshine.

Our gate area was filled with at least a hundred sunburned, strung-out stoners. And true to the stereotype, they looked tired, dirty, lazy, uninterested, unshaven, and unbathed. I've seen that look before—it says, "I don't care. Not about you, not about the rest of the world. Not about what you think about me. I only care about what brings me pleasure in the moment. Leave me alone."

There was a lesson from God here somewhere, if I could just find it.

∞

I didn't have to wait long. One of our team members, named Brad, said, "Hey, man, we have some time to kill before our flight leaves. Look at all these people! Let's go witness to them!"

Brad is big—his body, his words, his life, his faith. Everything about him is big. So I just followed his lead. He began each conversation cordially, with questions applicable to anyone. Where are you from? What do you do? How long were you in Goa? Nonthreatening and generic, they were the kinds of questions anyone would ask you in any similar situation.

But Brad's casual beginning quickly led to more serious inquiries. (We didn't have long, so he was evidently making the most of our allotted opportunity.) He began to ask them about their souls. What do you think about church? Do you have a Bible? Do you believe in God? What do you think about Jesus?

> How can you believe the Bible to be true? How can you know for sure you're right? What about all the other religions? And the best one of all: If God is a loving God, why is there so much suffering in the world?

The answers were as varied as the hairstyles of the hippies. Some of them were polite and gave us the hint by their body language that they didn't want to be proselytized. Others answered us in perfect English until Brad asked them about Jesus; then magically they could speak only Dutch. Others just ignored us altogether. But the final group we talked to was where I encountered God Almighty and learned a lesson straight from Him about belief, doubt, and the lost.

We were talking to a couple of guys from Denmark or Belgium (I can't remember now which). Their English was good, and they were kind and attentive. One was an X-ray technician and the other an anesthesiologist. So when the conversation turned to spiritual matters, these two well-educated Europeans had lots of questions about our beliefs and lots of reasons why they didn't agree with us. They had the common intellectual barriers to faith: How can you believe the Bible to be true? How can you know for sure you're right? What about all the other religions? And the best one of all: If God is a loving God, why is there so much suffering in the world?

Of course, there are no easy answers to these questions, and we weren't trying to offer any. We addressed these objections to faith at length, but to no avail. While some skeptics ask these tough questions out of a sincere desire to know the truth, others throw them at you like grenades in order to derail a conversation that's going to eventually turn to them—*their* sin, *their* guilt, *their* loneliness and isolation, and *their* deep inner desire to commune with the Divine and transcend the temporal world that has left them empty, even after a week on the beaches of Goa.

Our flight was about to board, and Brad posed a final question to the guys.

"Do you believe any of what I have said to be true?"

One of them replied, "No, I do not believe any of what you said is true."

And it seemed like an hour had been wasted. But his final comment, in its raw simplicity, spoke volumes.

"But I believe that *you* believe it."

And it hit me, standing there beside Brad, that sometimes that's all a person needs to see. Regardless of where they are in their lives or in their journey to or from God, if they can just tell that we really *believe* our beliefs, that impression will stick.

Brad ended the conversation respectfully and said something very profound (and, I believe, Spirit-led).

"I appreciate your listening to us. But just know this—you guys are young and have a lot of living yet to do. As you get older, life gets harder; things are taken from you, people you love lie to you, hurt you, and leave you, and the ones you love the most will die one day. And someday, you will wonder if any of this has meaning. You will wonder if this world is all there is, or if there's more. What you will need at that moment is something to believe in, something beyond yourself, bigger than you. You will scan your memory to see if there's anything in there to cling to. You will remember us and this conversation, and that we *really believed* in Christ. That will be enough to give you faith to believe too."

What an amazing way for God to show Himself! I think about those guys and pray for them even now. I believe they represent a world that finds us, our songs and meetings and clichés, very bizarre. So what the world needs now is not another airtight explanation of why our beliefs are right. They need to see that there's something compelling and true about Jesus, something that transforms our lives and deeds. And they will be drawn to Jesus if they see that we really believe.

9

Exemption—or Companion?

A man of many companions may come to ruin, but there is a friend who sticks closer than a brother.

—Proverbs 18:24

WHEN I WAS YOUNGER, I recall older folks, mostly moms and dads, talking about "how spoiled kids these days" were. I would get tired of hearing it. My own parents would talk about how my brother and I could have never survived in the world they'd lived in. You know, the one where they walked to school barefoot, uphill both ways, in a blizzard, fighting Apaches and polar bears. My parents and your parents likely went to the same school.

Once when my dad told me to get up on a Saturday morning to take out the trash, I complained I was sleepy and it was the only day I could sleep in. His response was typical. Mine was more insightful than I knew.

"Son, all you ever want is an exemption."

"No, Daddy, I don't want an exemption. I just want a companion. If you help me, I can get it done twice as fast!"

The struggles and losses of life can bring us to the point where we get worn down by the pressure and pull of this fallen world and we ask God for an exemption—a break, a vacation, a free pass. But that's seldom how God works. He offers us something much more tangible: a Companion. Instead of letting us avoid the valley of the shadow of death, He has us walk right through the middle of it...with Him by our side.

∞

My second son was born August 6, 2005, at about 6 a.m. The delivery was fairly quick, and as my wife recovered with a much-needed nap in her room, I ventured to the cafeteria to see what they offered for breakfast. It had been a long night, and my stomach was growling.

After I filled my tray with cereal, fruit, and coffee, I was surprised to see that nearly all the tables were occupied even at such an early hour. I stood there for a moment, just like a typical American, hoping to find an empty table where I could sit in isolation with plenty of my own space. There was nothing available.

But then I saw an older gentleman sitting at a table for two, eating his oatmeal under one of those blue baseball caps that war veterans wear, a cap that indicates where they fought or what naval carrier they were stationed on. I went right over and asked if I might share breakfast and conversation with him. He flashed me a big smile and said, "Sure, young man, sit right on down here!"

God will often bring us up close to individuals and circumstances for His own purpose. But if we're too busy with our schedules or agendas, or if we just choose to stay wrapped up in our own personal space or pursuit of pleasure, we'll miss out on amazing encounters ordained by God for our growth and His glory. Sometimes, though, I think God just decides that we absolutely must have that encounter. It's that important. So He aligns our circumstances in ways we can't predict and puts us in situations we can't escape.

He did in the cafeteria that morning. I had no choice. The only empty chair placed me in direct contact with this WWII veteran and, by God's design, in His sacred presence.

"So what are you doing here at the hospital?" I asked politely.

"Oh, my granddaughter just had a baby, and we are all up here with her."

"That's great! My wife just had our second baby boy about an hour ago. His name is Joseph," I replied.

And from that moment we hit it off like old friends. He was gentle and warm, much like the old men I grew up around—men like my grandfather and my uncles, and the gaggle of old saints who would stand around in a circle in front of the church talking every Sunday night after church services, until it got dark and the sound of the tree frogs drowned out their conversations.

The more we talked, the sadder I became just at the thought of how few men like him there were left in our world, how so many hundreds a day from his "Greatest Generation" were dying and taking their stories and memories with them. My own papa had died two years prior, and I missed him terribly. I'd felt a connection with the past through him, and especially to the terrible war that claimed so many millions of lives. When he died, he left a void in our family. Sitting there talking to this gracious gentleman gave me the sensation that God was giving me a few more moments with Papa. I would savor every word!

I have found his generation, especially veterans of WWII, to be humble and soft-spoken, and most often reluctant to talk about the war itself and the horrors they witnessed and experienced there. But I knew the kinds of questions to ask, and in just a few minutes, he was doing the talking and I was doing the listening. He talked about life on the farm as a little boy, picking cotton all day long and bringing water from the spring in a bucket. He told me about marrying his wife and leaving immediately for Europe, where he fought in France and eventually Germany.

When his mind turned to the war, he became visibly uneasy. His countenance changed from calm to tormented in the blink of an eye.

I wondered what memories were being dredged up in his mind at that moment to cause him such emotional pain. His words were syncopated with sighs, deep breaths, and silent pauses; from these, it seemed, he was deliberating about which words to use. I was overwhelmed with sorrow and admiration for this beautiful old soldier and prayed that my two sons, one of them just hours old, would never have to endure what this man had seen six decades earlier.

He gave few details about the battles and bullets themselves, but he did talk freely about one thing: his friends. And when he described them, his face lit up like a Christmas tree. Once the conversation turned to the men he had served alongside, the cadence of his words picked up, his smile grew wide and toothy, and the pitch of his voice became bright and happy. It was almost uncanny how total was his recall of so much personal information about these men.

From what I can remember, Jerry was from Omaha and had grown up on a corn farm; he had two kids who still lived in Nebraska. Johnny was an Apache Indian from Phoenix who had worked in the silver mines. He'd never married, which turned out to be a good thing. He was killed by mortar fire in the French countryside. There was Pauly from New York, the son of Italian immigrants, and Floyd from South Georgia, who'd farmed onions and watermelons until the draft took him away from home.

As my newfound friend told story after story about the men who'd made deep impressions on his soul, one thing became evident. He had loved them. And though most had died in battle or, back home, of the things that come with old age, when he spoke of these men, the light of love twinkled in his eyes.

"So how did you make it? How did you find the strength to survive those dark days?"

His reply was as simple as he was. "It was the men I fought with. They were the thing that got me through. They got me home safe.

"There were a lot of guys trying to get out of the war. They tried to make up excuses not to fight. I guess they wanted an exemption. But what I got was a whole lot better than an exemption. I got the companionship of the greatest men I have ever known, and I will never forget those men. Never."

A few moments later we shook hands and left the cafeteria for our families and newborns. I haven't seen him since, but the words he spoke have rattled around in my head since that humid August morning. He had described, in rare simplicity, what so many Christians struggle with.

When life gets hard, we want an exemption. We pray that God would miraculously swoop in and airlift us from the battle. What we hope for is to never experience the pain, the disappointments, and the losses of this life. We want insulation from the fallenness of humanity and isolation from the results of the sinfulness of mankind.

> If we got what we prayed for and God gave us an exemption from the harsh realities of life, we would be soft and spoiled and useless. And far worse, we would never need to lean on other people.

But God gives us something infinitely better than an exemption. He gives us a Companion. He Himself becomes our friend, a soldier in the foxhole beside us, a companion who's got our back in the heat of battle. He walks beside us in the darkest valley, and He sweats and suffers with us along the steepest and rockiest paths we walk. He never leaves us, never abandons us. He's always there, experiencing whatever loss or pain we feel.

At the end of the day, this is what the human soul craves. Not an easy road, but a friend on the hard road. Not an exemption, but a companion. If we got what we prayed for and God gave us an exemption from the harsh realities of life, we would be soft and spoiled and useless. And far worse, we would never need to lean on other people. We would never know the joy of a community of people who are there for us in grief. We would never know the warmth of a prayer or an embrace during seasons of brokenness. How pitiful and hopeless it would be to live an easy life and never need anything or anyone.

Thank God that in Christ we have a Companion who is faithful, trustworthy, and dependable.

10

Kill Your Idols

In the eighth year of his reign, while he was still young, he began to seek the God of his father David. In his twelfth year he began to purge Judah and Jerusalem of high places, Asherah poles, carved idols and cast images. Under his direction, the altars of the Baals were torn down.

—2 Chronicles 34:3-4

I love rock-and-roll. Not all of it, and certainly not the offensive, crude messages of many of the bands that perform it. But there's something raw and real about rock that I've always appreciated. And God showed me some really important things one day while I was watching one of the biggest rock concerts in history on TV.

I was at a friend's house during summer break, and it was too hot to go outside. The TV was on, tuned to MTV. Immediately I recognized who was playing, and I was drawn to the set and the man all the cameras were focused on. It was Axl Rose, the lead singer for the group Guns N' Roses. They were performing at an event in honor of the late Freddie Mercury, former lead singer of the rock group Queen, who had just passed away as a result of the AIDS virus.

It looked like Axl had a picture of a man on his shirt, and I was curious. He was moving around so much that I couldn't really make it out for a while. When he finally faced the crowd, I saw the words "Kill Your Idols." Underneath the words was a picture of Jesus Christ.

I don't know what the shirt meant to the millions of fans watching, but I remember what I thought. When I read those words and saw the picture of Christ below them, I was offended. But the phrase also brought to mind a story I'd read in the Bible about a young king who did just that. You could call this king an "idol killer."

King Josiah assumed the throne of Israel at the tender age of eight. His father had been a wicked man, but Josiah pleased the Lord and had a heart for God.

When the king was still a young man, he decreed that God's temple was to be cleaned out and sanctified so it could once again be used to worship. While this temple cleansing was taking place, the Law was found among the rubble by one of Josiah's friends.

He commanded that the Law be read to him. As he heard the words, his heart was pierced with sorrow and conviction. He ordered every false idol to be torn down, all pagan activity to cease, and every Israelite to repent and worship the one true God again. Not only did he tear down the idols and pagan places of worship, he also commanded they be smashed to pieces and ground into dust. He was determined to put an end to the things that brought God dishonor.

Josiah was absolutely serious in his quest to kill every idol exalted in Israel and to turn the heart of the people back to the one true God. If only we were this serious. We want to hide our idols. We want to compromise with our idols. We hold on to them, continuing to live a lazy life of apathy toward a God who says, "You will have no other gods before Me." Oh, if only we would grab them by the throat and murder them outright, devoid of any consideration except that of Christ, casting them to the ground, smashing them into dust, walking away from them forever.

Our day is a day of cultural and pleasure idols. We have not made graven images of gold. We have little plastic boxes with 198 channels or more, and golden chariots parked in five-car garages. We have bank accounts and investments, golf clubs and lake houses, satellite dishes and video games. Do we realize that these idols are just as offensive, pagan, and sinful to God as the statues Josiah cleansed from the temple? The idols we worship are just as forbidden today as they were then—not because they are evil in themselves, but because we allow them to take priority over our relationship with Jesus.

There's nothing wrong with material blessings that come from a life lived by faith in God's promises. There's no sin in wealth or possessions, until you begin to love them.

There's nothing wrong with material blessings that come from a life lived by faith in God's promises. There's no sin in wealth or possessions, until you begin to love them. When you love them, these things must die so that the place they have found in your heart does not become a cancer, an idolatry inching its way to your destruction.

It's been said, and I agree, that there's nothing sinful in possessing material blessings—until they possess you. The moment anything wrestles your affections away from Christ, it's an idol that must die. Josiah didn't confer with dozens of council members before he immediately set out to kill every idol. He eliminated every object that had taken the place of God in the temple of Israel and in the hearts of the people. Immediate action is required, and the only action to take is to smash our idols to smithereens.

Josiah's actions point to several thoughts. First, his heart was broken when he understood how Israel had displeased God. Many times we lack the ability to see our sin and not get defensive. Instead, we should weep with a bowed heart and bended knee, ready to take action and correct our ways.

Second, Josiah wanted the temple clean and spotless because it was the place where God dwelt. Josiah would not negotiate. He wanted to provide a pure place for God, so all the elements and remnants of paganism and idolatry had to go. If only we could grasp the truth that our bodies, minds, and hearts are the place where God lives! He desires a pure and holy dwelling within us, not one cluttered with lust and bitterness, or filled with worldly junk and religious trinkets. He wants us to maintain His dwelling—our heart—and keep it clean through the power of the Holy Spirit. Anything within us that opposes His supremacy must come down.

Third, Josiah didn't seek to bargain as we do. He didn't arrange a trade or work on a deal. He orchestrated a clean sweep. He left nothing as it was. No stone unturned. No idol unbroken. No secret place unclean.

∞

Imagine the benefits you would reap if you adopted this plan. Seriously, imagine! How you would change! How God would use you! How you would bring Him glory! If only we refused to be yoked to the idols of pleasure and culture, and settled only for total abandonment to Christ. Like Josiah realized in the case of the temple, some things must be destroyed before God can be supreme in our lives.

Don't ever forget that our God is jealous for His glory and jealous for us. He will not share His glory with worthless idols, nor will He share supremacy in our hearts with momentary illicit pleasures or fleeting sins. It's time for us, His children, to become aggressively serious about killing our idols.

We must stop anything in our lives that steals our complete affection for Christ—not just hide it away, but destroy it. It's not sufficient to place it on hold, or to shove it under the bed. We must throw it down and smash it to dust. Burn the bridge behind you and never come back. As long as you leave your idol in one piece, it will forever beckon you to return.

But once it has been ground to powder and pulverized, you can know the freedom of having destroyed that which had assumed a higher place in your life than God. You can know the freedom of encountering Him with no barriers between.

11

On Your Back

I am like a deaf man, who cannot hear, like a mute, who cannot open his mouth; I have become like a man who does not hear, whose mouth can offer no reply. I wait for you, O LORD*; you will answer, O Lord my God.*

—PSALM 38:13-15

THERE'S NO EMOTION QUITE LIKE the feeling of helplessness. Every time I feel it, it's horrifying. It touches our greatest fears, usually those of being in a situation that threatens pain or harm to us with no way of escape or protection. The most primordial fears—such as drowning, falling from a great height, or being buried alive—are all deeply rooted in the same overwhelming sense of needing help when there's none in sight.

I experienced this in Kenya in the mid-1990s when I contracted malaria. I was 21 years old, thousands of miles from home, wondering if I would ever make it out of the jungle alive, and that helped me take stock of my life and decide how I intended to live the rest of it—if there was a "rest of it" to be lived. But that story comes later in this book.

∽

God specializes in saving the day when we're flat on our backs, helpless to save ourselves. I pondered this one day at a mountain cabin in the Appalachians, watching my young son while the rest of the family was visiting friends.

I suppose I shouldn't be, but sometimes I'm still surprised when I encounter God and one of His great spiritual truths in a very ordinary scene. This time involved a simple ladybug.

My son Joseph, or Jo-Jo as we affectionately call him, was going through his two-year-old bug stage. I assume that all boys have a bug stage, some of them lasting longer than others. Jo-Jo spent a lot of time on the floor, exploring cracks and crevices, looking for living or dead things that piqued his curiosity; and usually he would bring them to me as proudly as if he'd bagged them on a hunting expedition to a faraway, exotic land. On this particular day he shrieked at me, in a tone full of earnest conviction, that I had to come into the den and see this bug on the floor. I obliged, as I usually do, without delay.

Upon arriving, I found Jo-Jo squatting over a ladybug. One solitary ladybug. He was talking fast, saying something about the insect being hurt and needing my help.

"Jo-Jo, what are you saying?"

"Daddy, dis wittle bug so hurt! It needs Daddy for helping it get up. It stuck on its back, you see it?"

"Jo-Jo, you can help it get up, just turn it over with your fingers."

"Oh, no Daddy, I scared of it; it will bite me and kill me. It's a scawey bug wif big teef!"

Though Jo-Jo couldn't get past the basic human fear of creepy-crawly insects, he had developed a sense of compassion for living things. Even at the tender age of two, he wanted his daddy to come and rescue this little bug, which was helplessly stuck on its back, unable to turn itself over. Jo-Jo and I sat there in the middle of the floor, and for some odd reason I was captivated by the smallness of the bug and its inability to help itself.

Out of nowhere, I saw the similarities between this bug and me unfold before my eyes. As I stared at the poor insect, I could relate to its feeling of helplessness; I often feel just like it—upside down, on my back, and unable to move unless someone bigger than me comes to my aid. I assume I'm so big and important, that so much in this world depends on me, and that I have some inner strength I can call upon in a time of crisis. But on my best day, after my most moving sermon or my most epic victory over temptation, I'm still seconds away from winding up flat on my back, looking up in hope for a compassionate God to lift me from the miry pit.

The most prudent thing for us is to immediately end our foolish pretense of ability and throw our hands up in surrender to our God.

I agree with the voices of the Reformers when they declare our absolute inability to do anything good, or worthy, in the power of our will or our flesh. The most prudent thing for us is to immediately end our foolish pretense of ability and throw our hands up in surrender to our God, in total dependence on His providence to get us off our backs and on the right footing again.

In the grand scheme of things, I'm but a speck in God's world, just a tiny speck He loves dearly and purchased from sin and death. If my two-year-old had a natural capacity to care about the outcome of a ladybug, how much more does God care about me and how I live my days on this earth?

And that goes for you too.

12

Dreaming of Jesus

He has made everything beautiful in its time. He has also set eternity in the hearts of men; yet they cannot fathom what God has done from beginning to end.

—Ecclesiastes 3:11

God is unpredictable. As soon as I think I have Him or His timing figured out, He decides to throw a monkey wrench in the whole thing—just to remind me that I'm not Him, perhaps, and to prove that He will not be preempted, figured out, or equaled in any way.

I guess that, as a preacher, I'm supposed to be the one who always trusts Him to come through. But I often doubt Him—I doubt His timing, His motives, His goodness, His love for me, and even His overall knowledge of the intricacies of any given situation.

But God never seems to be rattled by our inability to trust Him. He always has a plan, and it always works; and the more unlikely and surprising it is, the more likely He will get the glory for it (like when He used a stuttering murderer to save the nation of Israel from slavery, or a baby born of a virgin in a stable to save the world). My friend Richie proves this point quite clearly.

∽

I first met Richie in August 2008 in Malaysia—the thirtieth nation I'd set foot in since age 18. The trip was special for me on several fronts. But the event that stands out the most was what happened to this young Hindu man.

I was speaking at an international conference for university students in Kuala Lumpur, the capital. About 500 students had come there from China, Iran, Indonesia, Singapore, Kenya, Nigeria, Uganda, Saudi Arabia, and a dozen other nations. Over half the crowd was Hindu, Buddhist, or Muslim; the rest were Christian. I was in my element—engaging students from all over the world, many of them from countries I'd visited, and all of them with hearts and minds open to the truth. I would preach and then spend hours discussing the Christian faith, answering questions and debating the essence of truth.

Among several students who approached me after my Saturday morning message was a 20-year-old named Richie. He was a Malaysian and a Hindu, but he said he loved my preaching. The jokes and stories I told showed him, he said, that Christians had a sense of humor and knew how to enjoy life.

The conversation then turned to more serious fare—life and death and reincarnation, absolute truth and situational ethics—but our debate ended in a stalemate. He declared he could never convert to Christianity because of the discord and confusion it would cause his network of relatives and loved ones. I walked away thinking, *Well, Lord, maybe I planted a seed in his heart, but someone else will get to see it bear fruit—sometime far in the future, because he's not even close to being ready to give his life to You.*

∽

As I told you, God likes surprises.

That night I spoke for the last time at the student conference. I knew that many of those attending might never again be in a setting where they would hear the gospel and be given a chance to respond to it. I chose every word carefully, keenly aware of the strong contingency of Muslim students in the audience. (Two from Iran had actually gone into a private room before my sermon to pray to Allah for protection from my words about Jesus.)

The message was a simple, straightforward presentation of the facts about Jesus Christ: His life, death, resurrection, and return. I spoke of sin, repentance, and God's love, and boldly gave an invitation for students to convert to faith right there in the service. (The local ministers had encouraged me to go for it, and I did.) Thirty-three students indicated they had trusted Christ.

God puts His fingerprint on the human heart. There's a default mechanism deep inside each of us that turns to God, like a compass always points to magnetic north.

Looking over the group that came forward, I noticed Richie in the back row. During the final song, I made a beeline for him and asked, "Richie, what happened to you tonight?"

He replied, "I came in halfway through your sermon, and I felt Jesus grab my heart. My body was warm, and then hot, and I kept thinking about your words and how Jesus loved me. I could not stop shaking, and I am still shaking. And all I want to do is cry." His response was as genuine as I've ever seen.

"You repented of your sins tonight? You want to become a Christian?"

"Yes, I did give my life to Jesus, and I feel so happy and calm in my heart. I want to go tell my campus pastor, because he has been praying for me and talking to me about Jesus like you did earlier today."

As Richie walked away, I was flooded with emotions of thanksgiving and conviction. I'd assumed he was light-years away from faith, that it would take a lifetime for him to believe the gospel; yet God had already been preparing his heart. He had been saved just hours after we'd talked.

God still had one more surprise, though.

∽

Two days later we were all heading into the city, and Richie was with us. I lingered so we could talk for a little while. When he saw me, he strolled up beside me and said, "Clayton, can I tell you the rest of my testimony?"

I was all ears. But I wasn't prepared for what I would hear.

"When I became a Christian on Saturday night, many things had taken place before then. You know that I come from a Hindu family, and they will be very upset when I tell them I am a Christian now. But some time ago, my friend Tim invited me to church, and I went with him. That night I had a dream, and in that dream Jesus came to me. He didn't say anything to me; but He smiled at me, and He was surrounded by bright light. And in my dream, I knew that He loved me so much. He made me feel very safe and calm. I had peace all over my body, and all my fear and anxiety went away. Saturday night I could feel Him again, coming to me and giving me peace. Now I am a Christian, and I have the love of God."

Speechless and amazed, all I could do was laugh.

Isn't that just like God? He doesn't need me, or you, or anyone. His ways are beyond our ability to understand. He has gone before us, no matter where we tread or travel. Long before I set foot in Malaysia, Jesus had already been there, in Richie's dreams. And here I was assuming that this young man was far from God, when actually He was closer than his next breath.

God puts His fingerprint on the human heart. There's a default mechanism deep inside each of us that turns to God, like a compass always points to magnetic north. A moth is attracted to the light of a candle, and our souls are drawn to the Father God who created and designed us.

Richie's story reminds us not to make assumptions about how God will reveal Himself to those who need Him. And it reminds me that I'm not the only one who experiences amazing encounters with God. It also happens to Malaysian Hindus in their sleep.

13

Perishable Goods

Do not store up treasures for yourselves on earth, where moth and rust destroy and thieves break in and steal. But store up for yourselves treasures in heaven, where moth and rust do not destroy, and where thieves do not break in and steal. For where your treasure is, there will your heart be also.

—Matthew 6:19-21

ONE OF THE MOST VIVID MEMORIES I HAVE of my late grandfather was his frequent declaration, "You'll never see a hearse pulling a U-Haul." How true. But judging from the way many of us live, you would think we'd never considered this very true view on death and the accumulation of stuff.

Really, we value the wrong things in this world. It takes but a glance at our culture to prove this. Pre-born babies are murdered because they weren't planned and would be an inconvenience to a career-minded couple. However, this same couple will work themselves to death for a luxurious retirement devoid of the joy of children and grandchildren. We have turned our search for treasure upside down.

For Jesus, real worth was locked inside the human spirit, and real reward was bringing glory to His Father. He warned that earthly treasures had a short shelf life. If anyone was qualified on this issue, it was the Lord Himself. He had lived in both heaven and on earth and had seen the treasures of each. Knowing the worthlessness of working for perishable goods, He told us to invest in eternity.

> I simply embraced each of them with the love of Christ, picking up every child in my arms and kissing their forehead, laying my hands on every man and woman to pray for blessing and healing.

I've noticed that those who have the most earthly treasure tend to be the most reluctant to share it, while those who have little are quicker to part with it. Some people truly understand the concept of heavenly treasure. It's a long-standing mystery that philosophers and theologians have pondered for millennia: Why are the rich so stingy and the poor so generous?

While I can't answer that question, I can offer a personal reflection to illuminate the issue. Once again, God was waiting for me in the most unlikely place and in the form of a most unlikely person—waiting to peel back the dull colors of a mundane world and reveal to me the brilliant hues and shades of a sacred reality I'd never noticed before.

∽

One of my great international adventures led me to East Africa, where I spent my days traveling on foot from village to village, preaching in small churches and visiting the homes of the villagers. I would pray for the sick and share the gospel in every home I visited. I had an interpreter (who also became a close friend and brother) who went with me everywhere, teaching me about his culture and his people, and helping me communicate the gospel in every town.

Each village was similar. A small cluster of thatch-roofed huts made of mud, straw, and sticks usually surrounded a well. The population of most of these villages was about 50—fewer than a dozen families. The vast majority we visited had never seen a white person before, and the people I met were unlike any I myself had ever come in contact with.

They worked every day of their lives just to survive. Most had never owned a pair of shoes, and none had indoor plumbing. It reminded me of what America must have been like in the times of the pioneers. The most compelling characteristic of all the people by far, however, was their unbridled and immediate generosity, regardless of age or physical condition.

Sickness and physical deformities were commonplace. In almost any home I could expect to see a child with a cleft palate, a grandmother with a withered arm, or a father with a gigantic growth on his neck or face. These wonderful people had no access to doctors, hospitals, or medicine. Many died prematurely of easily treatable sicknesses or infections.

It was difficult to get so close to so many without the means or ability to treat them. I was left only with the regret that I couldn't take them home with me and get whatever it was that was wrong with them fixed. But since that was no option, I simply embraced each of them with the love of Christ, picking up every child in my arms and kissing their forehead, laying my hands on every man and woman to pray for blessing and healing, and enjoying whatever bit of food they could spare to honor their white guest. (What did it matter that the chicken meat was too tough to chew and had to be swallowed whole?)

I was unwittingly met by God as we entered the home of a very sick elderly woman. Of course, no one knew what ailed her, only that she was dying. She lived alone, having survived her husband. Her children attempted to care for her, but the inescapable poverty made it nearly impossible to feed both her and their own families. If she ate from day to day, it was as the result of charity from other villagers. Her diet consisted of boiled eggs, cassava (a starchy root), leftover ugali (African cornmeal mush), and water. And if nobody could spare food on a particular day, she ate nothing. She was literally skin and bones.

My interpreter and I entered her small mud home. She sat on a mat on the floor with both of her legs, atrophied and lifeless, under her. The only other material possessions in her hut were a small wicker basket, a metal bucket, a stool, and a towel. She was blind, so Isaac, my partner, told her who I was and why we had come—to pray for her, encourage her, and tell her about God's love.

This crippled and blind woman began to stir frantically. She pulled her emaciated body by one hand over to me, holding her other hand aloft as if asking for me to take it. I did. Then with my hand firmly inside hers, she slid over to the wall and plunged her free hand into the wicker basket. She dug under the towel that was inside it and pulled back her fist, obviously holding the treasure she was looking for.

In her hand she held one single egg. She opened my other hand and gently put the egg in my palm, and then she closed my fingers around it with hers and patted the back of my clutched fist three times as she smiled.

Isaac, my friend and interpreter, was in tears, because he knew this woman. He told me it was the only food she would have all day, and she had probably been saving it to eat before she fell asleep that night, since it was harder to rest on an empty stomach. She was honoring me as her guest and as a man of God.

I told him I would not dare take this egg from her! How could I be so greedy and shallow? It was all she had, and I wanted to give it back. This, however, Isaac told me, was out of the question, for I would have broken her heart by rejecting a gift so precious and valuable to her. It was more important to her that I be blessed than that she be fed. I did as I was told.

We prayed for her, laying our hands on her frail frame and feeling the bones of her shoulder through her shirt. She told us she was already a Christian, but she wanted me to share the gospel with her again. She wanted to hear an American tell her about Jesus before she died.

∽

What value does one egg have in our greed-driven economy? When compared to other earthly treasures, very little. But what value did that egg hold to me? It was priceless! I can't begin to express how that act of kindness touched me so deep inside.

I wasn't the only one blessed. Thousands have been blessed by this poor African woman's gift to me. When I relate this story to audiences all over the world, they wipe away tears. Her sacrifice has been multiplied, and it grows with each telling.

One person above all was blessed by the egg. It wasn't me, though I did eventually eat it. It wasn't the crowd of 5000 high school students who heard the story at a youth conference in Baton Rouge. It's not even you, as you read about it and imagine what she looked like as she scrambled to dig the egg out of the wicker basket in her mud hut.

The person most blessed was that woman, the one who gave away her egg. She was a living example of Proverbs 11:25, which says, "A generous man will prosper; he who refreshes others will himself be refreshed." Her only earthly treasure for the day was given to a stranger. But she knew her life was coming to a close, and she knew she could take that gift with her into eternity. She could lay that egg at the feet of Jesus, because in blessing a fellow servant of His, she blessed Him.

What small treasures we possess can be multiplied once we let them go! This woman's account in heaven was full. When she put the egg into my hand, her face was a vision of happiness and contentment. I only regret that I didn't have my camera to take a picture of her smile. But I know I'll see it, and her, one day in the kingdom, for her heart's treasure was in heaven and not in this world.

As Isaac and I left that village and walked the eight miles back to where I was sleeping, the sun disappeared behind the acacia trees, and the air grew cool. I still had the egg in my hand, because I feared it would break if I put it in my bag. Isaac noticed I was carrying it and asked me if I liked eggs.

"Oh yes, I like eggs very much. But this one...it's my favorite egg, the best egg I've ever had." A thousand years cannot wipe that sacred encounter from my heart, nor the lesson God taught me as I met one of His saints.

14

Beneath the Surface

Do not judge, or you too will be judged. For in the same way you judge others, you will be judged, and with the measure you use, it will be measured to you.

—MATTHEW 7:1-2

THEY HAD OVERSOLD THE FLIGHT, and I was bumped to first class. I settled into the much larger, more comfortable seat, hoping to close my eyes and not open them until we landed in Dallas. I wasn't really expecting to have a God-ordained conversation with a very angry person. But if we train our eyes and ears to look for God, even in the least expected places, we see the reality of His presence there too…even in the pain and bitterness of those who have been run over by life.

He sat down abruptly, with no regard for my hope of a nap, and immediately started talking loudly. He smelled of alcohol and cigarettes, and was dressed like someone who thought he was more important than he really was. I just knew from the get-go that God had put us together on that flight, and He'd given me a first-class seat to make sure of it. Thanks, Lord.

My new neighbor quickly informed me he was an investment banker in "the city" (which is code for New York City). He was a headhunter, making calls and sealing deals daily. His name was respected, his firm was in the top tier, and he got offers weekly to take higher-paying jobs.

I admit I was irritated by his arrogance. But something sacred was brewing, and so I was waiting for the right moment to introduce the spiritual realm into this very unspiritual and draining conversation.

The moment finally came when he asked me what I did for a living. I simply responded with "I'm a minister." On hearing those words, he was transformed into a different man—his face flushed, he pressed his lips together and squinted his eyes. And there was enough venom in the words that followed to poison a nation. I won't repeat exactly what he said to me, but it was ugly and mean. Here's a G-rated version of an R-rated tirade.

"A minister? Man, I hate all of you guys. You all make me sick. You go around telling everybody how to live their lives, what they aren't allowed to do, and then you take everyone's money. I got you figured out. I know your angle—you're all a lousy bunch of liars and thieves! I hope you all burn in the hell that you try to scare the rest of us with."

I've learned something very simple about people in over 20 years of ministry. It's this: No matter what mood you may see someone in, or how he or she might react to a situation, there's *always* something more going on beneath the surface.

The big-city banker was taking out his rage on me, though I'd never had any hand in ruining his life. But somewhere, someone had. I wanted to find out who—and more importantly, what—had scarred him so deeply.

"It's pretty obvious that someone has hurt or disappointed you in the past, and I'd bet they claimed to be a Christian. Whatever it was, I'm truly sorry it's affected you like this. What happened to you?"

He was more than prepared to unload all the bottled-up bitterness, and I had no choice but to sit there and take it. After all, I'd asked for it. And I did sense something very raw and real taking place—I felt like I was locked into a sacred encounter with someone God loved dearly, but who was unable to see His love because of this ugly hatred he carried around.

He told me that he (along with numerous other boys) had been sexually abused by his priest while serving as an altar boy in his hometown church. The man had told them all to keep quiet or something bad would happen to them and their families. God would punish them for getting the priest into trouble.

I've learned over the years that silence is sometimes better than words, so I obliged his request and prayed that God would do a miracle.

Not only had this man grown up associating God with the priest who molested him, but he also believed that God had sanctioned the abuse and would mete out severe retribution if he told even one soul. So to him, God was evil—perverted, secretive, vindictive, taking pleasure in harming little boys. No matter that none of this was true. He believed it to be true because of his experience.

What could I say at a moment like that, ripe with rage, tension, and years of misunderstanding and resentment? With great fear and trembling, I said the only thing I could think of, in the hope that God would break through. I told the man that God didn't approve of such things, that the priest didn't represent God or Christianity, and that God Himself loved him and wanted to heal him of this terrible hurt.

∞

I wish I had a happier ending for you, but truth be told, that was the end of the conversation. My seatmate told me he didn't want to hear my sermonizing. I've learned over the years that silence is sometimes better than words, so I obliged his request and prayed that God would do a miracle.

There was no way I could have known, when he sat down beside me in my unexpected first-class location, that he had harbored such a destructive secret all those years. And I wonder how many times every day I bump into folks just like him and never know what has gone on, or is going on, under the surface. I'm so quick to lash out, bite back, shake a fist, or give a rude person a piece of my mind without ever considering what unspeakable calamity they might have undergone. This is one of God's lessons to me.

God offers us patience, mercy, and grace, because He has the advantage of knowing every single thing we have been through. We would do well to practice more of His patience with people...because if we could take a glimpse into their lives, their marriages, their jobs, their past failures, their broken relationships, their regrets and disappointments, we would most likely embrace them with gentleness and meekness, instead of meeting their venom with some of our own.

There's always more than meets the eye. And God's presence is always there. So maybe I can give people some room, and some grace, before I think I have it all figured out. Jesus did, and He was a pretty good example.

15

Providence

My God will meet all your needs according
to his glorious riches in Christ Jesus.

—Philippians 4:19

IT'S NO SECRET THAT I BELIEVE GOD lurks behind every rock and tree with something to say to us. He has spoken clearly and perfectly in Scripture and in Jesus. And He continues to speak to us, never contradicting His two perfect revelations, but expanding on what He's already revealed—like a daddy who continues to tell his children he loves them, even though he's already told them thousands of times.

Now, some of the stories I share in this book look like a real stretch. For example, it's not easy to see God in falling down a flight of stairs in front of an admiring audience. But the following story is no stretch. It took place in one of my favorite places, a place I believe God is fond of too.

It's not that hard to encounter God at the Grand Canyon. It was there that He surprised my two companions and me by showing that He's never caught off guard, and that we're never far from His providence.

℘

My first trip to this unutterably beautiful natural wonder took place in 1994. I was about to enter my senior year of college and had a full summer planned. I was preaching all over the country at camps, churches, and conferences, but in the midst of all our other summer busyness I'd conspired with two of my closest friends to make a trip to the Grand Canyon.

The only thing we planned was our destination. Everything up to that point was up in the air and would have to play out as it happened. What could one expect from three guys no older than 20, full of vigor and vitality? There was a giant hole in the surface of the earth approximately 2400 miles away, and it beckoned us to come and conquer it. We intended to heed its primal call, rise to the challenge and, with juvenile naiveté, disappear over the ledge on one side and emerge battered but victorious on the other.

In other words, we were typical dumb college jocks with no idea what we were doing. We did no research whatsoever, had no clue how to get there or what the terrain was like—or that the temperature in the bottom of the canyon in June hovered around a comfortable 115 degrees.

℘

I flew to Dallas, where I joined my friend Trey. He and I then drove to Albuquerque to pick up Loring, the final member of our triumvirate. And, we struck out west, hoping to come to a dead end where the road stopped and the surface of the earth dropped away beneath our feet.

Since we could read a road map, we found the South Rim of the Grand Canyon. Some nice people at a convenience store told us we would need permits to hike into the canyon overnight. When we told them we weren't going to spend the night but intended to hike to the bottom and back out in one day, they gave us the look that said, "We'll be seeing your rescue story on the evening news!" They told us we would never get permits for the next day, or probably anytime for the next six months.

Trey and Loring glanced at me, clearly thinking we had just wasted a trip across the country. But I responded with conviction, "Guys, there's nothing to worry about. God is going to take care of us. We are going to hike the Grand Canyon before we leave."

When we walked into the ranger station and asked for three overnight permits, the ranger laughed out loud at us! I wanted to know what was so funny, and he told us that permits had been sold out for the next nine to twelve months. For the rest of the summer, there was no chance at all that we could spend the night inside the canyon on the South Rim.

Dejected, we walked out, and as we stepped off the porch, he yelled at us to try the North Rim ranger station. It was less popular and more out of the way, he said, so they might have some permits—we could get there in about five hours.

When we got into the truck, I confidently assured my two buddies, "Guys, there's nothing to worry about. God is going to take care of us. We are going to hike the Grand Canyon before we leave."

∽

Five hours later we arrived at the North Rim in a steady rainstorm. We went to the only hotel there and asked if they had any rooms available for the night, since it was getting dark soon.

"You're joking, right?" was the response from the desk clerk. "The North Rim Lodge books rooms 18 months in advance, and before you even ask, there's no chance of a cancellation tonight."

Things looked bleak. I looked at my buddies once more. "God is going to take care of us, guys, and will find us a place to stay tonight. Then tomorrow we are hiking the Grand Canyon."

In what little daylight was left, we drove to the ranger station, hoping against all hope that they had three backcountry permits for the next day. Amazingly, they had exactly three, so we left with renewed hope that our dream would come true.

We just had to find a place to sleep that night, since the tent that one of us had packed turned out to have more holes in it than a pack of Swiss cheese. The tent option was out.

We drove a few miles to a gas station. None of us had a cell phone in the stone ages of the mid-1990s, so we found a pay phone and started calling around to try to find a hotel nearby. We didn't get any further, because the guy at the gas station told us the closest hotel to the North Rim was three hours away, and it would certainly be booked up. We decided to call anyway. And he was right.

> Our conversation was filled with laughter and a few concessions from my friends that maybe there was indeed a God and that He did listen to the prayers of His people.

So we had permits for the next day but nowhere to sleep in the rain, except a tent riddled with holes.

I distinctly remember walking out of that gas station under an awning and hearing the screen door slam behind me. The guys had begun to panic, and one of them said to me sarcastically, "Well, if God is going to take care of us tonight, He'd better be quick about it, because we are out of options."

At that very moment a white Pontiac pulled up to one of the gas pumps under the awning. It was literally coming to a stop as the three of us walked out the door. Then a young lady hopped out of the driver's side, looked straight at me, and said words I'll never forget.

"Stop right there. You are Clayton King, and I know you!"

I had no idea who she was. It was half dark, and I was two breaths away from deciding we would just spend the night in the truck. So the three of us stood there dumbfounded, waiting for the mystery girl to tell us who she was. The answer came immediately.

"You look like you don't remember me. Well, Mr. King, you and I had a class together when we were freshmen. We had that swimming class, and you were always so loud and crazy. Remember me now? I'm Nina!"

Then I remembered! We had said "hi" a few times, but she was always quiet; and quiet types seemed to avoid me when I was younger. She started running toward me, and when she got there, she gave me a giant bear hug like we were old school friends who hadn't seen each other since third grade. My buddies were just looking on in disbelief.

"What are you guys doing out here in Arizona?" she asked.

"We're here for the Grand Canyon—why else would we be here?" I responded.

"Wow, that is so cool! That's what we're doing here too! We're hanging out for a few days until we hit the trail." She pointed back at the Pontiac, and her two cousins climbed out of the car.

"So you guys absolutely must let us buy you dinner tonight! We have reservations at the North Rim Lodge overlooking the canyon in 30 minutes. We were on our way there when I saw you standing in the door over there, and I thought I'd pull over and say hi."

Trey and Loring were smiling at me now. Maybe they'd begun to believe that God was watching out for us after all.

We followed them to the lodge, and our conversation was filled with laughter and a few concessions from my friends that maybe there was indeed a God and that He did listen to the prayers of His people.

Then my Texas friend said, "But you know, if He really loved us, He would get us a dry place to stay tonight."

∞

At the lodge, our group sat down at a giant table right beside the window. The sky had cleared and the sun had just gone below the horizon. Between the north rim and the clouds was the most beautiful mixture of orange, pink, purple, and red the human eye had ever seen. We watched the colors shift and change as darkness settled in.

Just as they handed us menus to order from, Nina looked at me and asked, "So where are you guys staying tonight?"

The three of us looked at one another simultaneously. Grins were exchanged, and there was a momentary pause. Then I answered for all of us.

"Well, that's a good question, because we aren't sure about that yet. See, we really didn't plan this trip that well. Actually, we didn't plan it at all! We just thought we would go straight to the Grand Canyon, walk down into it and back out, and that would be it. But there are no rooms available, and our tent has holes in it. And—" Then she interrupted me.

"Oh, you guys have to stay with us! We have a huge cabin with two extra bedrooms. It was the only thing available when we decided to come out here, and so we took it. We would love to have you guys stay."

It was completely dark outside, the closest hotel was three hours away, and anyway, it had no rooms available. All day long I'd been telling my two closest friends that God would take care of us—that we would find a place to stay and that we would get permits to hike into the canyon. It was all going to work out. At least that was what I was saying with my mouth. I hoped that God heard me.

The bottom line is that God is trustworthy. No matter how He chooses to do so, He provides for His children.

He did. And He arranged circumstances in a completely unpredictable way, in a way we would have never dreamed. He waited to the last minute and sent someone from as far away as we had come, not only to give us a dry place to stay, but also to buy our supper.

I know this story has a happy ending, and I don't want to give the impression that God will always intervene like this in every situation every single time. But that doesn't change the fact that He did it this time. We slept warm and dry with full bellies that night.

∞

The bottom line is that God is trustworthy. No matter how He chooses to do so, He provides for His children. It may be a miraculous last-minute save, it may seem that He has forgotten you and your request. But ultimately He comes through, for His own purposes and by His own means, for His glory and our growth.

We must keep on believing in Him. We must tell ourselves, and the naysayers around us, that God will save the day. It doesn't matter if they believe us, or even if we believe ourselves. After all, it's Him we're believing in—that He will come through, even if it's in a way completely different from what we prayed for. Eventually God wins, and we see His providence. In the meantime, we just keep believing.

16

Raise Your Hand If You've Ever Held a Severed Arm

STRANGE TITLE FOR A CHAPTER IN A BOOK, I KNOW. But it's a surefire way to gain the attention of a roomful of people or an audience I am about to speak to. Yes, from time to time, I do ask this question. And most of the time I am the only person who raises my hand.

As I've told you, God and I have a history—He speaks to me, I reluctantly listen and obey, and He shows His glory and proves to me He had a good reason to give me some strange, unexplainable desire to do something that seemed to have no practical purpose. As happened again in April of 2009.

It was a Thursday. About lunchtime. I was hungry. I had spoken the previous night in Arkansas. Had flown into Charlotte, North Carolina, early that morning. Skipped breakfast because it was too early to eat and drove straight to a public school assembly. Spoke to a thousand students about life choices and consequences. By noon, I was starving. Hungry enough to eat tofu. (And that, my friends, is hungry.)

With food on my mind, I was pulling into the parking lot of a church very close to the school. I was going to surprise a friend who was the pastor by asking him to lunch. My treat. He didn't know I was coming. I was excited to see him, to catch up, and to eat lots of food. Did I mention I was really hungry?

As I turned in, I felt a strong compulsion that I needed to go straight home—skip lunch, don't surprise the pastor, just drive directly to my house. It was unexpected and seemed to spring up from nowhere. But it's a scenario familiar to me. It often means that God is trying to get my attention. He wants to reposition me, move me to a different location so I'll be ready for what is going to happen in that other place.

This is one of the many benefits of being God. He can see the future before it happens. I cannot. Why would God want me to go home now, an hour's drive from Charlotte? What was so important there that God would stir up in me an unmistakable urge to change my plans and follow His? And what about food?

I told God I was okay where I was. I informed Him I had made personal plans for the afternoon. I reminded Him of how I love to help and encourage pastors, pray for them, and buy them a meal.

While I was setting God straight (and my stomach was rumbling with discontent), my phone rang. I glanced down and saw it was my wife. Figured I'd better answer it since we were married and everything. Her exact words after I said hello were, "I think you need to come straight home right now." It seemed she and God had been talking. There was nothing pressing, no emergency—she simply wanted me to come home because she hadn't seen me in so long. (My wife is convincing. And almost always right about everything. No kidding.)

Even though I didn't want to, I pulled right on through the parking lot and back onto the road that would take me home. I was a little ticked off. I'd been looking forward to catching up with this pastor. And eating. It didn't take long, however, to figure out exactly why God wanted me back at home that afternoon.

When I arrived, it was afternoon nap time and all was quiet. Feeling like I should have stayed with my original plan of lunch in Charlotte, I decided to join the family and plopped onto the couch myself.

I had been asleep for less than ten minutes when I was jolted awake by a very loud hammering at the front door. I staggered over, unsure if this was a dream or real life, and when I got there, one of the neighbor children was standing there, sweaty and out of breath.

"Clayton, come quick! We had an accident and Mama sent me down here to get you." He was calm and direct and gave no indication that anything really serious had happened. Our gravel driveway is a half-mile long, so we hopped into my truck and sped toward the main road, where he said their car had "run off in the ditch."

> "Mandy, are you okay? Did you hit your head?" In a million years, I would have never guessed her response.

So I arrived on the scene expecting a basic, ordinary wreck. And that's what it looked like. Their SUV had veered off the pavement and run off into the bushes and trees beyond the grass. There were no other cars involved. The vehicle was still upright. It had not flipped or rolled over. It was sitting still. No smoke. So I walked over to the passenger side door, opened it, and climbed into the passenger seat. Mandy, my neighbor, had been driving. She was still sitting behind the wheel when I sat down beside her.

Something wasn't right.

Having grown up on a farm and bagged my share of deer and bear (yes, I have taken several black bear), I recognized the smell of blood.

It's unmistakable. It rushed over me and into my nostrils the moment I climbed in...but there was none anywhere on the dash, seat, or steering wheel. I looked sideways at Mandy and asked her the usual kind of question.

"Mandy, are you okay? Did you hit your head?"

In a million years, I would have never guessed her response.

"Clayton, I've cut my arm off!"

She looked me directly in the eyes as she said those words. I leaned forward and looked toward the driver's side door.

Her arm was gone.

It had been severed about six inches below her shoulder. Her window had been smashed and was no longer there. As my eyes traveled further, I saw blood everywhere.

And on the ground a few yards from their car was her arm.

✑

Mandy had been coming home with her four kids from school and had fallen asleep less than half a mile from their house. The car slowly crossed the middle of the road, veered into a ditch, and hit some small trees. All the while her left arm was resting on the window ledge. When the car hit a tree, the impact broke out the window and her arm fell limp outside the car. She woke up, but it was too late. The vehicle was scraping against a pine tree, and as it slid, her arm was severed.

When she came to and realized she'd been hurt, she heard God speak to her. He told her to undo her seat belt and wrap it around her upper arm. So she made a tourniquet out of the belt and told her oldest son to run to my house and get me. Then she sat there. And waited. And prayed.

When I realized what had happened, my adrenaline levels spiked. I could feel the surge of physical strength and mental clarity sweep over me, and I became hyperfocused on the need at hand. I grabbed the seat belt to hold it tight. Mandy's right hand was shaking and weak—a few more seconds and she would have been unable to hold on any longer. I held on firmly. I prayed with her. Sang for her. Quoted Bible verses. Kept her mind off things.

Some neighbors came and took the children. The ambulance arrived about 20 minutes later. I told the paramedics what had happened and how long it had been. They took over, and I hopped out of the SUV with one thing in mind: *I have to get her arm!*

I jumped into my truck and took off back down my driveway like a NASCAR champ. I grabbed the biggest cooler I could find in our garage, washed it out, and filled it with cold water and all the ice we had. My wife was awake by now, and she went with me.

I knew it would be some kind of miracle if they could figure out a way to make it work again.

When we got back to the car, someone said there was no use getting her arm. It would be impossible to save it. I simply replied that if it were one of us, we would want our arm to go with us to the hospital. That seemed to settle things. One of the medical personnel actually agreed.

So I picked up her arm, cleaned it off, and placed it in the cooler.

I know what you're wondering. Of course it felt weird! Yes, it was creepy. Yes, it was sort of clammy and cold to the touch. But I had enough adrenaline coursing through my body to fight off a horde of Mongol marauders. I think I handled it pretty well, considering the situation.

As the ambulance left, someone asked me if I thought they could re-attach Mandy's arm and if she could ever use it again. I said honestly that it would be nearly impossible. Her arm had been detached from her body for more than an hour. I'm no medical professional, but I knew it would be some kind of miracle if they could figure out a way to make it work again.

Good thing God knows how to do miracles.

∞

After weeks in the hospital, dozens of operations and procedures, and lots of prayer, Mandy's arm was successfully re-attached. Though one of the nation's premier surgeons took on the challenge, Mandy was warned not to expect much in the way of recovery. It would take years and years for nerves to grow back. Infection would be a constant fear. She would be on antibiotics for months. Her body could easily reject the limb. And even if that didn't happen, it was very unlikely she would ever get feeling back in her hand and fingers, much less be able to move her arm or use it in any way.

But she proved them all wrong. With an unwavering trust in God's ability to do the impossible, Mandy followed orders; she went to therapy and did as she was told. She kept praying and telling about God's provision and protection. Every TV interviewer, every newspaper reporter, every person who asked her what had happened or how she was doing heard the story of how God had spared her life, protected her children, and allowed her to keep her arm.

∞

At the writing of this story, the accident is just 15 months in the past. Mandy is still years away from the point where even the most generous prediction would have come about of her being able to move her arm at all. Yet just days ago, I pulled into her family's driveway to say hello and watched her lift her arm, raise her hand, and wiggle her fingers. She can even bounce an exercise ball. She has smashed every expectation and amazed everyone who had an opinion about her situation. And she just keeps talking about how good God was to let her live that day. She magnifies the Lord, gives Him the credit, and continually honors Him at every juncture, every interview, and every opportunity.

My role in this whole thing was very small. But I would have missed it if I hadn't heeded God's unmistakable nudge to go home. So I intend to keep listening to God. And obeying what He says.

And wouldn't you say this qualifies as an amazing encounter with Him? Raise *your* hand if you've ever held a severed arm!

Yep, that's what I thought.

17

God Still Raises the Dead

FROM THE TIME I WAS A SMALL CHILD, I've always been drawn to stories of adventure. Whether it was Huckleberry Finn and Tom Sawyer rafting on the Mississippi or Indiana Jones searching for the lost Ark of the Covenant, as soon as the adventure began in a book or movie or cartoon, I was sucked in...completely and totally. To this day I'm still that way, and so are my two boys. I guess they got it from me.

So it should be no surprise that at age 25, when a friend invited me to help lead a 50-mile backpacking trek into the Himalayas to reach a people group who had never heard the message of the gospel...and told me we could be killed if we were caught by the wrong people...I immediately said yes.

From that journey to a remote region of North India on the border of Pakistan comes the story I'm about to tell you. If I'd been an atheist, this happening would have immediately convinced me there was a God.

I recruited a handful of young, single guy friends of mine to accompany me. We would attempt to backpack into a few small Tibetan Buddhist villages in the region of Ladakh. As far as we knew, if we were able to reach the Zanskar Valley by traveling along the Kashmiri border with Pakistan, we would be the first missionaries to ever reach that area. Our plan was to pack in medicine and equipment for small, mobile medical clinics. While we were there in those villages, we would hand out copies of the Bible in the local language, as well as comic-style books with pictures of major biblical themes and stories for those who couldn't read or write. We were warned very clearly, however, that there was fierce fighting between the Indians and Pakistanis along the border and that when we drove through Kashmir, and particularly a small town called Kargil, there was a very real chance we could be bombed, taken hostage, held for ransom, or killed.

We were warned very clearly that there was...a very real chance we could be bombed, taken hostage, held for ransom, or killed.

My five friends and I spent all summer long training, running, hiking with heavy backpacks, and taking ice-cold showers in our attempt to prepare for the adventure that awaited us. We lost weight and drank nothing but water. We read books on Tibetan Buddhism, and we prayed and fasted for God to make a way for us to get to the Zanskar Valley, and particularly to a small village called Zangla, which was as remote as it was legendary for being a place missionaries had never reached. (Remember the name of that village. It will be very important. You will see why soon.)

The time finally came. We flew into one of the highest airports in the world, Leh—over 11,000 feet above sea level. The air was paper-thin and breathing was painful. We acclimated for a few days in Leh, dealt with the jet lag, and tried to drink as much water as our bodies could hold in order to hydrate ourselves for the trip. After a few days, we loaded our gear (medical supplies, tents, backpacks, Bibles, and Bible storybooks) into a large vehicle that would carry us all the way past the town of Kargil, which sat on the Indian side of the border with Pakistan. We were told that if we were going to be killed, it would be in Kargil. That was good to know.

Every day we prayed for God to make a way for us to get to the Zanskar valley. We asked for miracles. We were willing to die, though not particularly excited about the prospect. And we were praying specifically that we could take the gospel, along with our mobile medical clinic, to the village of Zangla.

We approached the place we feared most after several days on the road. And as we got closer to Kargil we saw a plume of black smoke rising. Directly across the river was a ridge of high mountains. This was the disputed territory between India and Pakistan, and it was controlled by bands of Islamic militants—Pakistanis who wanted the region of Kashmir to break away from Indian control. They were known to be ruthless and aggressive, and it was these fundamentalists we had been warned about. Just months before we arrived, four European missionaries had been caught by one such group while smuggling 11 Bibles in their backpacks. They had been executed. We had 1100 Bibles and storybooks with us in Rubbermaid containers. We were sitting on top of them in our vehicle. And on the outside of each box, written in big black letters, was the word B-I-B-L-E-S. In other words, if we got caught, we would be in some big trouble.

We were stopped by an Indian soldier with a very big gun who refused to let us go into Kargil. He told us the town had just been bombed from across the river, which is where the plume of black smoke was coming from. After some prayer, some conversation, and a small gift of 40 rupees, the soldier agreed to let our vehicle pass. We drove right past the buildings that had been bombed just moments earlier. People lay dead. We wondered if the attackers would launch more mortar fire while we were there. But we had a flat tire, and Kargil was the only place to get it fixed before we continued toward Zangla. We had no choice but to stop and wait.

Here's where things begin to get unbelievable, so pay attention.

We rushed out of town once the tire was fixed, hurrying to beat any more mortar attacks. As we were leaving, our driver pulled over to the side of the road to pick up a hitchhiker. I immediately protested.

None of us knew this man, and he could have been a terrorist rigged with explosives for all we knew. The driver told me to be quiet, that he did indeed know the man, and that he was a very important personage. As a matter of fact, he was royalty—a real-life king.

Absurd! I became more upset and raised my voice, demanding that this man get out of our vehicle. Our lives were in danger, we had just seen dead bodies dragged from a building, and we were targets for terrorists (1100 Bibles sort of gave us away). There was no way this man was a king. While I was talking, the hitchhiker looked over at me and said, in broken English, "You are a very loud-talking boy."

Wow, this just kept getting better. Now the guy spoke English. So I turned to him directly and said, "Sir, I am sorry, but if you are really a king, what are you the king of, and why are you standing on the side of the road trying to hitch a ride? A king should have his own car, right?"

Now it gets *really* good. He replied, "My name is Raja Norbu, and I am the king of the Zanskar Valley. I live in a small village called Zangla. It is very far from here and difficult to reach. As provincial governor, I must attend annual meetings in the capital of Delhi. I was on my way there when my vehicle broke down. Your driver recognized me as King Norbu. That is why he is giving me a lift."

Silence. We all looked at each other dumbfounded. There was no way he could have been making this up. He claimed to be king of the very place we were trying to go, and our driver knew this was true, which is why he was willing to risk picking up someone we thought was a total stranger. This man could give us permission to take the gospel to his village!

Then he asked me my name. When I answered, "My name is Clayton King," his eyes lit up and he clasped his hands together like an excited little child and said, "Oh, my friend, yes, you are also a king in your country! You are very big and strong, like a king!" Because my last name was King, and because in his culture a person's last name indicates their vocation or identity, he assumed I was a king, literally. When he asked me what we were doing in Kargil of all places, I told him the truth. I told him we were actually on our way to his region, his village, to hold free medical clinics and give people our holy book, the Bible.

He evidently liked the idea, and took out a pen and asked for a piece of paper. In a show of respect and hospitality, he then wrote a personal letter and handed it to me. I asked him what it said because it was written in Ladakhi. He said, "My friend, I want you and your people to go to Zangla without any trouble. This letter will ensure you safe passage there if anyone tries to stop you. Give this letter to my wife. She will take care of you. I have written that you are going to be the King of Zanskar until I return from Delhi next month."

Yep. That happened. To honor me as a visiting king from America, he made me the king of his region, guaranteed us safe passage to his village, and instructed his wife to give us whatever we needed for our medical clinic. How in the world...?

↜

Several days later we arrived in Zangla on foot. It was hot and dry. My feet had blisters and my back hurt from the pack I carried. The Himalayas towered on both sides of the valley and the village clung to the edge of a cliff, a small place of fewer than 100 people. They were all very poor by Western standards and lived in small huts made of mud, dung, and sticks.

I found the queen by showing the letter to the first man I met. When we reached the right place, a woman came out to meet me. She told me that Raja Norbu had two wives and I needed to speak with the older one. So the two women took me into their home, a modest house that was a little bigger than the rest, with a few simple furnishings, but certainly not a palace of any sort. They made me butter tea and gave me some crackers, and then they bowed and welcomed me as the new King of Zangla. I still couldn't believe this was happening.

She asked the strangest question anyone had ever asked me. "Raja, do you know how to deliver a baby?"

Our team set up camp right outside the village. We slept like dead men that night and rose early the next morning to hold the medical clinic. There was a steady stream of people all day long as we treated everything from boils to cysts to pneumonia. And Ladakhi children are just like kids in America—they love wearing Band-Aids.

We made fast friends with everyone who came that day. As the sun sank behind the snowcapped peaks, we began to pack up our gear. Then I caught sight of the older queen, the one with the authority, walking toward our tents. She had a strange look on her face.

She said, "Did you have a good day today helping my people? Did you have everything you needed?" I assured her we were delighted to be there and appreciated her kindness and hospitality. When I paused, she asked the strangest question anyone had ever asked me. "Raja, do you know how to deliver a baby?"

Of course I had no idea how to deliver a baby. I'd seen it done on *Little House on the Prairie,* so I knew you needed to boil water and get clean sheets. And that was all I knew. However, we had a medical doctor on our team who had delivered babies before. As a matter of fact, she worked in a hospital emergency room, so she had seen just about everything. When I told the queen, she said we needed to come quickly because one of the village women had been in labor for more than a day and they feared she would die soon.

We left two of the guys back at camp to watch our stuff, and the rest of us put on our headlamps, grabbed some supplies, and followed the queen to a small hut. Dozens of people were gathered, burning incense, chanting prayers, and walking about the room. In the corner was a tiny Ladakhi woman lying on sacks and blankets. Blood and water were on the floor. The villagers were taking their Tibetan scriptures and touching them to her head while chanting prayers.

Our doctor, Abby, examined the mother and told us she was pregnant with twins and the first baby was breeched. That was why she couldn't give birth. And if Abby couldn't turn the baby soon and get the twins out, the mother would die from dehydration. There was also a good chance that the first baby was already dead in the womb. Then she asked us all to pray, because the villagers were very superstitious—if the mother or babies died, they might think we brought that bad luck upon them and perhaps do us harm or kill us in their anger.

∞

So there we were. All the way across the planet. We'd made it to Zangla. Had God really brought us that far to fail? To be killed? Had God really allowed me to be named the interim King of the Zanskar Valley so we could get there and share the gospel...only to have this mother die in childbirth and the villagers blame us?

By this time the entire village had arrived to see if our God could do what we'd said. We had told them all about Him in the clinic. We had given them Bibles and spoken of the power of Jesus. Could it be that God was allowing us to now show them His power, immediately after we'd told them who He was? I assumed that this was exactly what He was doing, so I prayed out loud, asking our driver to interpret it to everyone who had gathered in the room and at the door and windows.

"Tell them we have come from America as the people of God. Our God is Jesus Christ, who was killed for our sins and then raised from the dead. He's powerful and loving, and He will show you His power.

This mother will live tonight. And these babies will live tonight. God sent us to you for this purpose. If they die, then you can do with us anything you wish." I heard myself saying those words but couldn't remember actually planning out any of them in my head. I then wondered what would happen if the baby was already dead in the womb. Well, too late now. God would do whatever He wanted to do, and we would be there to see the results.

Abby had to break the first baby's leg at the hip to get him to turn before she could deliver him. And when he was born, we all held our breath. He was dead. There was no telling how long he'd been that way. No breath, no pulse, no heartbeat. Nothing. And we were on the hook for it.

> Jesus had a plan of His own that nobody else could understand. He always does.

I panicked and began praying for God to get us out of there alive, to do something to fix this situation. The rest of the team was also praying while all the villagers watched. And as we were praying, I heard a baby scream. I looked down, and the little baby boy who'd been born dead was screaming at the top of his lungs in Abby's arms. He was alive! God had raised that baby from the dead and the entire village had seen it happen.

I took off my shirt and Abby wrapped him up in it. Then she splinted his broken hip with duct tape and Popsicle sticks. Not long after that the other little boy was born. He was fine and healthy. We gave the mother an IV drip, and she fell asleep on the floor while the women of the village took the babies and tended to them. We packed up our gear and received the many thanks of the villagers who had just witnessed this miracle. Though it was very late when we got back to camp—around midnight—I didn't sleep that night. I lay outside my tent looking at the stars, my body filled with adrenaline and my heart about to burst with the thought of what we had just seen God do among these people. *He had raised the dead.*

∽

I kept thinking about the story of Lazarus in the Gospel of John. Jesus knew Lazarus was sick and could have healed him before he died. Yet He waited two days to go to His friend, and by the time He arrived, Lazarus was already dead. This made no sense to the friends and family. They all loved Lazarus. Didn't Jesus? Why did He let him die? Why didn't He just cure him or heal him? Yet Jesus had a plan of His own that nobody else could understand. He always does.

The people knew Jesus could heal the sick. They had seen Him do it. That's why they had sent a messenger asking Him to come quickly, while Lazarus was still alive. They wanted Jesus to make him well before it was too late. However, the Son of God wanted to show them something new, something they had never seen. He wanted them to know that not only could He heal the sick, He could also raise the dead. So He waited. He waited until all hope was lost. Then, in His own time, He went to the tomb and revealed the power and the glory of God by calling a dead man from the grave, giving him life.

Jesus raised the dead. And He still does, spiritually and, in this case, physically.

The people of Zangla are Tibetan Buddhist. They don't believe in God or a god, but they fear evil spirits and demons. They are animistic and superstitious. Often in cultures like theirs, the most effective way for the gospel to be made clear is through what missiologists call "a show of power." This is where the traditional form of religious belief comes head-to-head with the proclamation of the gospel that Jesus is Lord. Traditional spiritists cultures respond to the power, or the god, who can prove himself or itself as most powerful in a showdown. They want to know and serve the real god, the most powerful one.

I believe that is exactly what happened in that village. The people had never heard of Jesus. We show up out of nowhere and tell them there is a God (a foreign idea to them), that His name is Jesus, and that He is more powerful than the demons and spirits that they fear and burn incense to ward off. Then, within a few hours, God provides an opportunity for them to actually see in their own lives what we had just proclaimed to them. They were praying and chanting and reciting their mantras in hopes of ridding the mother of evil spirits they believed would harm her or her babies, but their methods weren't working. Then, we came to the house. And we told them our God would show Himself to them. And though it would have been just as easy for Him to let the first baby be delivered healthy, it would not have made the same impression on the villagers as it did when the baby was born dead and they then saw God bring him back to life as we prayed.

Jesus could easily have healed Lazarus. He could have done it from a distance. But what would show God's glory in an even greater way? Letting Lazarus die and then bringing him to life in front of an entire village full of witnesses.

∽

I'd never seen anything so amazing before that night in August of 1998. I haven't seen anything that can compare to it since. And I may never see it surpassed in this life as I consider all my amazing encounters with God. But I'm always looking for the next encounter, when God surprises me out of nowhere when I least expect it. Maybe you should be paying closer attention too. You never know when God may show up and remind you that He's always right there.

18

The Stench of Self-Regard

Do not think of yourself more highly than you ought, but rather think of yourself with sober judgment, in accordance with the measure of faith God has given you.

—Romans 12:3

I have to admit, there are times I want to stand up straight, clear my throat, take a deep breath, swallow hard, and scream as loud as I can to the people around me: "IT'S NOT ABOUT YOU!" People need to hear this from time to time, because judging by the way most of them act, you'd think they believe this world revolves around them. It's sinful to think such ridiculous thoughts.

Paul admonishes the Roman believers to think soberly about themselves. To paraphrase, he essentially tells them to take an honest look at themselves. Some call this reflection. Some call it a sabbatical. Others refer to it as "finding themselves." The one necessary element to "think of yourself with sober judgment" is that a person must actually look inward...and not consider the appearance they project to those outside. This can be disheartening, frightening, and enlightening.

This is the exact reason our world is filled with so many noises and distractions. Anything that keeps us from conducting honest, inward reflection seems good and desirable because it diverts our attention from our insecurities and fears. If you don't believe me, try going an entire day without music, television, phone conversations, or time on the computer. It would drive some people mad.

> As I strutted past the front desk, I overheard them talking. (Actually, I strained to hear.) "That's Clayton King! He lives in Shelby, and I heard that he comes in here sometimes. But I've never seen him up close. Wow!"

Let me mention some practical ways believers can look at themselves honestly and soberly. First, keep a journal of your spiritual growth. Be totally honest, and do not hold back. Let your heart flow onto the page. Read what you write and look at yourself with a critical eye. Ask yourself whether or not you're growing into the disciple you want to become.

We can also ask the Holy Spirit to reveal the truth about us to ourselves. But be warned—He can and He will. There's nothing more sickening than when God shows me my sin by revealing His own beauty and holiness to me in an unmistakable way. It's placing a priceless diamond next to a lump of coal. No comparison exists.

∽

If we really want to think of ourselves properly, we must leave the pretend world of super-inflated self-image. Instead of believing what we say about ourselves, we should ask others what *they* think about us. Of course, if you have the guts to actually give others access to your life and the courage to ask them to correct and rebuke you, then you need to ask God to give you the backbone and thick skin to stand up under the weight of truth.

I do this. I ask a small number of people to be brutally honest with me no matter what. They balance out what I think about myself with the truth of who and what I really am.

Really, our problem is not that we dislike ourselves, but rather that we love ourselves too much. If a person really hated himself, then his thoughts would not be consumed with ways to improve his appearance or increase his popularity. If he really hated himself, he would *want* to be ugly and unpopular. (That's what we would want for someone we hated, right?)

In reality, poor self-esteem in many cases is a masked version of self-love. Self-love causes a person to turn too much attention inward and have a high regard for himself without input from outside sources. How foolish.

⁓

God has hilarious ways of reminding me that it's not about me. Recently I was on this kick about church members who leave churches because they are "not being fed" (which I'd decided was a secret code for "not being entertained"). I was foaming at the mouth, high on my "it's-not-about-you" horse, and I was on my way to preach my "it's-not-about-you" sermon at a local college campus.

I stopped by a music store to buy guitar strings. When I walked in, I noticed two girls whispering behind the counter. I figured out that one of the girls was telling her friend she recognized me. As I strutted past the front desk, I overheard them talking. (Actually, I strained to hear.)

"That's Clayton King! He lives in Shelby, and I heard that he comes in here sometimes. But I've never seen him up close. Wow!"

"Yeah," her friend replied. "I've heard him preach so many times, and he's really funny! I wonder if he's friendly or stuck up?"

The important thing was that they'd recognized me!

The stench of self-regard must have permeated the first floor of the store as I sauntered past them, pretending not to notice I was the object of their conversation. I bounded up the stairs to the second floor and got my strings, anticipating the conversation that awaited me at the cash register. I would act surprised when the young woman asked me if I was Clayton King, play it down, and then leave as proud as a rooster.

But as I started down the stairs from the second floor, I tripped. And fell. It was obvious, and it was loud. Everyone in the store saw and heard. I groaned aloud in embarrassment and tried to play it off. But now, instead of two people, there were about ten onlookers—afraid to laugh because they thought I might be hurt.

As I fell, all the ideas I'd been rehearsing in my mind on the "it's-not-about-me" sermon came crashing down on top of me. Then I heard one clear voice laughing. I looked around to see who it was, but no one's mouth was moving. I realized that the laughter I heard was coming from God. He must think it's ridiculous when we parade through life like we are the greatest gift to the human race.

I picked myself up and went to the counter to pay, and the two young ladies were still there, caught somewhere between pity and hilarity. I tried not to look them in the eye.

"Are you okay?"

"Oh yeah, I'm fine—I just lost my balance a little bit."

"Well, I was wondering, because you're bleeding pretty badly."

And sure enough, I looked down and saw that my elbow was gashed and blood was running down my arm. I paid for the strings and tried to get my handkerchief out to hold over the cut.

"Are you Clayton King?" the other girl asked.

And with God's laughter still ringing in my ears I said, "Yes. Unfortunately."

19

Growth in the Low Places

He said to me, "My grace is sufficient for you, for my power is made perfect in weakness." Therefore I will boast all the more gladly about my weaknesses, so that Christ's power may rest on me.

—2 CORINTHIANS 12:9

IT WOULD BE NICE IF EVERY DAY could be a good day, especially if God let us order it in advance. Life would be so much easier if I knew that next Thursday was going to be partly cloudy with a high of 65, that I would spend two hours on the phone and an hour returning e-mails, that my kids would respond "yes, sir" to my every request, and that my wife would prepare my favorite dish for supper.

But we don't have the luxury of all good days. (As a matter of fact, before I finished the first paragraph of this chapter, I was interrupted by my wife telling me that our two-year-old had painted all over the walls and floor in our room. I spent the next half hour cleaning that up!) I know of no place in the universe where we can custom-order our days.

Would we really want to?

Not only would it take all the spontaneity out of life; it would also remove all unknowns, taking away our opportunity to grow through adversity and difficulty. After all, it's usually when things go poorly that we turn to God for help. It's in the dark times of life, when we feel abandoned or hopeless, that we fall on our knees and beg God for a miracle. The low places in life, not the high ones, are the most fertile soil for spiritual and personal growth.

I see the same principle at work in the natural order of the outside world, a place where God speaks to me, and has since I was a boy. Things will grow only in certain places under certain conditions. God showed me this lesson on a backpacking trip in college.

℘

I was a senior and had already finished most of my required courses; I'd planned it this way so I could coast through my last year taking easy electives. One such class was "Outdoor Education," essentially a course on hiking and camping. We learned how to pack, what boots to wear, what foods to take, how to set up camp, and what kind of socks were best on your feet. But the element of the class I loved most was the field experience: We put what we learned into practice by hiking and camping in the Smokies.

It was April, and we had a trip planned near Clingman's Dome. We had been to Linville Gorge earlier and had gotten snowed in pretty badly. But I had already forgotten how quickly cold weather can move in; instead of packing heavier and more cumbersome warm clothes, I decided to pack light so I could move faster on the trail than the rest of the class. My vanity and stupidity at that age still baffle me today.

It was 70 degrees when we left campus, so why would I possibly need gloves or insulated underwear? When we disembarked at the trailhead, I was in shorts and a cotton T-shirt, nothing else.

The trail headed straight up to a shelter called Ice Water Springs. After an hour the wind began to blow in from the north with a bitter sting.

An hour after that, snow flurries began. With every step I tried to convince myself it would blow over and warm up. But we were going up, not down—and in the higher elevations it was certain to only get colder.

As we moved uphill the trees got smaller and smaller. By the time sundown approached, there were only scrubs and bushes. We got to the shelter, and everyone was chilled; but due to my carelessness in not packing layers, I was really suffering. We quickly set up camp, and began searching for something to make a fire. There was none. (No trees, no firewood.) We had to hike back down the trail and drag some dead limbs up to the shelter before we could get a fire going. Flames never felt so good.

All night we shivered in our sleeping bags. The next morning we awoke to four inches of snow on the ground and a howling wind that seemed to blow right into our faces. I put on every stitch of clothing I had and figured on a pretty miserable day. My hands were so cold that I put my extra pair of wool socks on them to keep from getting frostbite. It became apparent to all of us that if we didn't get moving, hypothermia would set in.

At that altitude, the wind was blistering and snow was blowing from every direction. At a few spots it was almost a whiteout. I began to wonder if we would ever get off the mountain alive. All the worst-case scenarios went through my mind, and I prayed that we wouldn't be lost in the snowstorm and freeze to death huddled under a spruce tree.

At about 11:30 that morning, the trail began to descend. We had been meandering around on the summit for several hours, but once the trail turned downward and we moved to a lower elevation, the wind began to subside. I also noticed the air warming up. And the snow stopped. My fingers that had gone numb began to ache with the return of feeling, and I was thankful for the pain in them. Everyone's spirits began to climb as we descended. We were going to make it.

We were hiking to Kephart Shelter, several thousand feet below Ice Water Springs Shelter. At about two o'clock I saw butterflies! The sharp contrast from our icy lodgings the previous night made me keenly aware of all the sources of life lower down. The sun was shining brightly—the poplar, spruce, and white pine trees were gigantic. The entire Pisgah National Forest smelled alive. The dirt smelled good, the trees smelled good, the air was musky with the scents of spring, and I'd never been so happy to feel the sun warm my cold flesh.

We have to get off the mountain because just below us is work that needs to be done, people that need to be cared for, and lessons from God that need to be learned.

When we finally arrived at our campsite, the whole group was buzzing with the kind of feeling that comes after it seems like you've cheated death. We talked about how cold it had been last night, how most of our tenderfoot friends back on campus would never have survived the ordeal, and how tough we all were. After a late lunch most everyone dozed in the warm sun beside the nearby creek. I decided to take a stroll on an old logging road I'd noticed beyond where we'd camped.

The road climbed about 200 feet to a beautiful vista overlooking our camp and the creek. From one point—a warm perch on a tree stump—I could see the campsite below us, but I also had a clear view of the mountain we'd shivered on the night before. It seemed like a dream...I remembered the cold and panic I felt, but the fear and the isolation were gone; I was safe in a low valley where the creek teemed with fish, gnats and flies swarmed around our lunch, and giant hemlocks stood like towers over the trail.

It was at that moment God spoke very clearly to me in my heart. If I had to put it into words, here is what I heard Him say:

My son, pay attention to what you see. Above you is a lifeless, barren mountaintop. Below you is a fertile valley filled with life. Nothing grows on the top of a mountain. Life is found in the low places, in bottomlands, where the soil is fertile and deep and rich.

I pulled out my pocket journal and began to write furiously. I didn't want to forget this.

And since that day, I've drawn strength from what I learned. Though my desire is to dwell on mountaintops, where things seem simple and the views are gorgeous, there's not enough on a mountaintop to sustain life. The soil is too rocky and the air is too thin for anything to grow and thrive. Like the disciples who wanted to build shelters and spend the night on the glorious mountaintop where Jesus had just met with Moses and Elijah, I always want to stay where I won't grow.

But Jesus speaks to me today like He spoke to them back then. We have to get off the mountain because just below us is work that needs to be done, people that need to be cared for, and lessons from God that need to be learned. Down in the valley, where the sun is warm and the air sweet with moisture, things are alive and growing.

Now I look forward to the occasional trip up the trail to a stony peak, but I always yearn to get back to the bottom to be surrounded by living things, and by opportunities for me to grow along with the rest of them.

20

Jets and Jesus

...Having a form of godliness but denying its power.

—2 Timothy 3:5

If you spend as much time on airplanes as I do, you've probably spent some time thinking about the aircraft themselves. There are things an airplane offers its passengers that I feel certain I'll never need. For instance, seat cushions. They are extremely uncomfortable for one thing. But they have a second purpose: They also float. Yep. As in water. Here is the commonly heard announcement that the FAA requires be made on every flight before takeoff:

> In the unlikely event of a water landing, your seat cushion can be used as a flotation device. Simply reach down, pull your seat cushion away from your seat, and place your arms through the straps, clutching the flotation device close to your chest.

My favorite word in that announcement is "simply." Everything is simple—until your plane crashes in the water! But in a crash, will I really need a flotation device at all? When I fly from Charlotte to Memphis, I don't need something that floats—I need something that will bounce when my plane drops into a parking lot or a cornfield. So I really don't see the need for a floaty.

The world we live in finds Jesus about as useless as I consider airline seat cushions. In the West we have strong economies (even in bad times, we are super-wealthy compared to the rest of the world). We have high literacy rates, ample edible food, reliable transportation systems, and compulsory education. We have access to medicine and health care, even if it's not always affordable for those with less money. We have a stable democracy backed by a strong military.

I could keep going, but you get the point. When things are so predictable and convenient (we get water from a faucet, when a Ugandan mother walks eight miles a day to fill her gallon jug for her family of six), we don't really feel we need God or the things He offers us. We are too obsessed with the here and now to worry about sacred and spiritual things. After all, who needs the spiritual and intangible when we have the convenient and concrete?

∽

Which brings me back to airplanes. It's never brought me even the slightest bit of comfort when the flight attendant reminds us to fasten our seat belts tightly around our waists. If the jet is going down (and with the help of gravity begins to reach speeds that would make Superman look like a slowpoke), am I supposed to feel good about being strapped tightly to a 30-ton metal rocket filled with jet fuel?

So again, just like people who really see no need for Jesus (because they have never really needed Him in a pinch), I've never seen the need for a seat belt on a plane.

Or at least I didn't until...*turbulence.* That's a little word that gets thrown around frequently in regard to air travel. I pride myself in being immune to it. I've never once been airsick. I'm a skydiver and have even flown a small plane once myself (with the help of the pilot). So whenever a plane I was in hit a rough spot and skipped about, I would remain calm while all the novice fliers were gasping for breath. I would always keep my composure, and I chalked that up to experience. But that was before the worst flight I'd ever had—on May 26, 2008, a date I can't forget.

Between Charlotte, North Carolina, and Fort Smith, Arkansas, we flew straight into a thunderstorm. And it was wilder than any roller coaster I'd ever been on. We hit a cloud, and the bottom fell out from under us. We dropped like a rock—and I shrieked like a girl!

But it got worse. The plane turned sideways and stayed that way for a long time. The pilot couldn't get it straightened out, and it felt just like a car when it fishtails. Then we dropped again, but way worse than the first time.

That was when I realized why we needed seat belts. Two people didn't have theirs on, and their heads smacked the overhead luggage compartments the way Hank Aaron smacked baseballs. But while they were head-butting those hard plastic panels, I remained in my seat (the cushion of which, by the way, can be used as a flotation device). Why? My seat belt.

∽

Jesus does not appeal to many because they see no immediate need for Him. We postmodern Westerners are a very practical cut of humans; if we don't really want or need something immediately, we usually ignore it. And I fear that this is one of our greatest faults. Unless Jesus can save us 15 percent on our car insurance or help us lose some weight, we're likely to ignore Him like we ignore the fine print in a contract or the extra 30 pounds sitting around our middles.

We don't start paying attention until we reach a critical mass. We don't start losing weight until we get diabetes, and then it's way too late. We don't want to spend time with our kids until they have grown up and moved across the country with their own children. We don't start eating better and exercising until our cholesterol is through the roof.

And this is the apparent similarity between Jesus and jets. There are safety accessories in a jet just in case we need them. In other words, they're for emergencies. People think of Jesus this way. He's a safety net in case we fall. He's a cosmic Santa Claus that gives us stuff if we're good, or a spiritual superhero who swoops in to save the day when we are powerless to save ourselves.

Jesus is not there to simply offer us a feeling of safety and assurance. If that's all we ever get from Him, we have missed the point entirely.

It's astonishing the number of individuals I've seen on airplanes performing the Catholic ritual of crossing themselves during takeoff or landing. Yet when I ask if they are Christians, I often get this reply: "Oh no, not really. I just want to make sure I have all my bases covered, in case of an emergency or something."

And that is where the similarity between Jesus and jets ends. The Lord Jesus is like a seat belt to an extent—He offers safety in a time of turbulence. But that is not His priority in how He relates to us.

Christ is the very Lord of the entire universe, so to treat Him as nothing more than a backup, a last resort when all else fails, is to miss the point—and also the joy! The unspeakable joy of being set in a right relationship with the Power who thought me up, created me, and sustains me every single moment is unlike any emotional or physical euphoria in this world.

I just wish those silly people who make the sign of the cross before a flight, or who cling to a religious trinket like a spiritual good-luck charm, could see how close they are to the Reality that is God, the God who can save them from drowning in their own sin and who can hold them tight when the storms of life blow in around them.

Jesus is not there to simply offer us a feeling of safety and assurance. If that's all we ever get from Him, we have missed the point entirely.

Jesus is to be loved, experienced, worshipped, and known! His wisdom and goodness are unfathomable, but He can be known by the smallest of children and the simplest of faith. May we not miss the divine joy of friendship with Christ because we think He's only a utility device in case of an emergency.

21

Epiphany

"What about you?" he asked. "Who do you say I am?" Simon Peter answered, "You are the Christ, the Son of the living God." Jesus replied, "Blessed are you, Simon son of Jonah, for this was not revealed to you by man, but by my Father in heaven."

—Matthew 16:16-17

PEOPLE ARE FILLED WITH REASONS WHY they don't believe in Christ as Lord. In over two decades as an evangelist I've heard every conceivable reason, legitimate or made up, why people won't give over control of their lives to Jesus.

"If God is loving, then why is there so much suffering in the world?"

"How can one religion be right and all the other ones be wrong?"

"How do we know for sure that Jesus really did all that the Bible claims?"

"The Bible was written by people and is full of errors, so why trust it?"

"I don't want to be close-minded by choosing such a narrow belief."

"I need to get back in church, but I'm just so busy."

"The church is full of hypocrites and sinners; why do I need it?"

To believe He loves me means I did nothing to earn or deserve it–it's a free gift He initiated. I can take no credit in the exchange.

"I want to make sure I'm ready to be a Christian, and I'm not ready now."

"I'll get things right eventually, but probably when I'm older."

All these reasons, and the countless others people give, are honestly not the major objection to faith. The real roadblock, I believe, is a simple one: Human beings have difficulty believing that God really loves them—period.

It's not an intellectual hurdle as much as it is an emotional one. Accepting the love of God goes against our self-sufficiency and offends our pride. To believe He loves me means I did nothing to earn or deserve it—it's a free gift He initiated. I can take no credit in the exchange. God has never owed me anything, but loves me regardless. He never will owe me anything, but He will keep loving me anyway.

There's a deep and broken part of me that doesn't know how to handle that sort of perfect, unconditional love. So it's really the love of God we have the hardest time with, not all the arguments and smoke-screen objections.

∞

But little children don't have that problem. Why is that? Why do kids trust so easily and love so quickly? Though I can't explain the intricacies of the preadolescent psyche, I do feel qualified to speak about children since I have a couple that roam my house every day.

From the time my boys were born, my wife and I have told them that God loves them. We say it, sing it, and remind them of it constantly. But more importantly, we try to show God's love by loving them and loving each other. We pray that one day, instead of just hearing us say that God loves them, they'll begin believing it. We want it to "click" in their hearts so the understanding is theirs, not just something Mama and Daddy said was true.

So many young men and women abandon the faith of their families when they go off to college or out on their own. Some of them never return. Others come back to faith and to church when they have kids of their own—either from genuine conviction or from a sense of nostalgia, wanting their children to have the same experiences they had. We'll never know who really is saved and who is not; that is for God to know and sort out one day.

Nonetheless, our American culture is full of adults who walk away from faith in Christ. Their faith was never *their* faith; it belonged to someone else.

The old story rings true: A young man who had been training to be a monk approached the father of the monastery and told him he doubted God and had lost his faith. The older father just smiled and replied, "No, my son, you have not lost your faith. You have lost your *parents'* faith. Now go find your own."

We hope and pray that our boys have such a genuine relationship with the Lord that they never need to walk away from it in order to find it again.

∞

One morning I was taking Jacob to preschool. It was just the two of us in the truck. He was barely four years old, and just like every morning we were singing songs. We were halfway through one of his favorite songs, "Jesus Loves the Little Children," when Jacob had that *moment*—that flash of insight where the love of God becomes more than a cute concept or a line in a song. We were singing these words:

Jesus loves the little children,
All the children of the world.
Red and yellow, black and white,
They are precious in His sight,
Jesus loves the little children of the world.

Jacob began yelling from his car seat, "Daddy, Daddy! I understand something!"

"What, Jacob—what do you understand?"

"Daddy, Jesus loves the little children, and I am a little children. That means that Jesus loves *me!*"

And right there in my Ford Escape at the stop sign on Burke Road and Highway 150, I experienced one of the most sacred moments in my life. My own son, my flesh and blood, had felt the love of God, not just for all the little children in the world, but for him. My firstborn son had been touched by the power of the gospel, and I was right there with him when it happened. I felt God Almighty sitting in the car with us.

∞

It's more than innocence that makes little children so close to the heart of Jesus. It's their willingness to trust in the goodness of others. They're so unaware of themselves that they don't even know they bring nothing to the table! The kids Jesus held in His arms and blessed were too swept away with being loved and noticed to worry about whether or not they were worthy, or deserving, or good enough. Children aren't like us grown-ups. They don't struggle with coming to God empty-handed. They are too enraptured with His love to even notice. In that respect, I want to be a child in the eyes of God, resting in His affection, trusting in His goodness and love for me.

To return to my opening thought, it's not the intellectual hurdles that harm and hamper a robust and compelling faith and keep it from developing in us. It's the emotional hurdle of believing the unquestionable *fact* that God cares for us deeply—that He was crazy about *you* to a degree that transcends logic, that He poured out His mercy on you and me by offering the supreme sacrifice—the life of His only Son. He has no other agenda. He is love.

And it takes the faith of a child to trust that this is true.

22

Obedience and the IRS

I HEARD ABOUT GOD from the time I was adopted by my parents, when I was just a few weeks old. I knew all the stories about Him from the Bible. I learned them in church, at Sunday school, and from my parents. But I didn't surrender my life to God until I was 14. That was when the reality of what Jesus did for me on the cross became tangible.

When Christ saved me from my sin, I got serious about God's business. I wanted to know Him and follow Him. I wanted to encounter God on a regular basis and show others how to have an encounter with Him. And I found that when I got serious about His business, He got serious about His blessings. I've seen this play out dozens of times.

God will impress an idea on my heart. He will tell me to do something that looks crazy on paper. I argue with Him and give Him all the reasons why it won't work. Or I just convince myself that it wasn't God who told me to do it in the first place. Instead, it was an idea I came up with. Then I try to forget it. What shows me that it was God who spoke to me is this: The idea will not go away—it just keeps getting stronger.

Here's one story to illustrate the importance of simply obeying God when He tells you to do something. The way this all went down left no doubt whatsoever that He was trying to teach me a lesson. He made it as clear as day.

It happened like this.

In the mid-1990s, a young lady named Sarah was part of one of our India mission teams. She was 17 when she made her first journey to this beautiful country, and she was by far the youngest person in our group. Yet from the first time I met her, I knew God had placed a very special calling on her life. One of eight children, she was very mature for her age. While at the orphanage where we were living in India, she told us she intended to go back to America, graduate from high school, raise some money, and move back. She wanted to learn the language, graduate from Bible college there, marry an Indian pastor, and start her own school and orphanage.

If any other 17-year-old had said this, we would have laughed. But not Sarah. We fully believed she would do exactly what she said she would do.

And she did. Exactly as she predicted. I attended her wedding in India in 2001, when she married Rabi. The two of them started an amazing ministry in his home state serving the poor, lepers, orphans, and their community. In turn, my wife, Charie, and I began supporting their efforts to train young men and women for ministry. And when Sarah and Rabi would travel back to the U.S. to raise funds or to visit her family, we would always plan to see them or have them stay in our home.

They happened to be coming through our town during one of these trips home, and we were going to eat lunch with them, catch up on what was happening in their ministry, and give them some money to help with all they were doing for Christ. We were supposed to meet for lunch at noon on a Wednesday.

I'd already decided I was going to give them $100. Things were tight financially in the King home. We had a little baby boy. We had spent some money remodeling part of our house. We had some home repairs that couldn't wait and they cost more than we had expected. So for me, a $100 gift was fairly significant. It was, in my opinion, a sacrificial gift, one we would feel. I felt pretty smug about it. And I hoped God would take notice of our generosity and perhaps make it up to me later at some time when I was in a budget crunch.

When you're dealing with God, you cannot be obedient in installments. He wasn't interested in negotiating with me. I guess that's one of the benefits of being God... you don't ever have to compromise. Your ideas are always perfect.

ൟ

The night before we were supposed to eat lunch with our friends, I was sitting at my desk catching up on some work, when I saw the checkbook, which reminded me I needed to go ahead and write the check for $100. Immediately, the very second I thought about the check, I'm sure I heard God speak audibly to me. And in my heart, I heard the Holy Spirit say, *I want you to give them $1000.*

At first I shrugged it off as just a stray thought. I would discard it and stick to the plan. This was ridiculous. We couldn't afford it. It was ten times the amount I'd decided on. But it wouldn't go away. As a matter of fact, the sense that I *must make out* the check for $1000 became more compelling. Next I protested. I told God, and myself, that it was a ludicrous thought. We didn't have much more than that in the bank. As the wage earner in our family, I had a fiduciary responsibility to provide for the basic needs of the other three people in my household. Giving away $1000 right now would be irresponsible and reckless.

Yet the more I protested, the louder God's voice became. I felt my skin getting hot on my face. My heartbeat sped up. Then I decided to bargain with God. It was my last card to play since ignoring His message and protesting hadn't worked. I explained to Him that I had a three-year-old and a six-month-old. I told Him I'd just paid cash for a minivan so we wouldn't have to borrow money at a high interest rate, and it had left us running on fumes in our checking account. So I tried to cut a deal. I promised Him that as soon as we reached a more stable place financially, I would write the check. Or even better, I could pay it in installments. I would give the $100 check as planned and then send Sarah and Rabi $100 a month for the next nine months.

But when you're dealing with God, you cannot be obedient in installments. He wasn't interested in negotiating with me. I guess that's one of the benefits of being God (not that I would know)—you don't ever have to compromise. Your ideas are always perfect. No holes, no blind spots, no wild cards. So when God tells us to do something, if we really trust that He's already thought the whole thing through and not only sees the outcome but *guides* the outcome, the best plan is to just shut up and obey Him.

I have difficulty doing this.

If you're like me at all, you probably do too. We tend to be humanly pragmatic. We want to see God's plan from start to finish before we buy in. We want guarantees and assurances and ironclad promises that if we obey Him, every little thing will work out exactly how *we* want it to. For my part, I delay and wait and make excuses and waste lots of time trying to make sure there's a safety net big enough to catch me if I obey God and He lets me slip. This is my pattern.

Yet ultimately, when I reluctantly come kicking, screaming, protesting, and whining to a hard-won place of obedience, the very second I do the thing God has told me to do (either in Scripture or in my spirit), I feel a sense of calm pour over my nervous heart. The act of moving forward, even in fear, seems to unleash a sense of God's presence. Faith is not an attitude. Faith is an action. I don't really believe a thing until I *do* that thing. I don't really believe God until I have *obeyed* God.

So the issue is obedience. Plain and simple. Old-fashioned obedience. Doing what God tells me to do means I believe God did what He said He did in Jesus.

∞

Sitting there at my desk with my checkbook in hand, listening to God tell me I needed to give a gift ten times bigger than the one I'd already planned to give, and in full knowledge of how tight our money was, I gave in. Even though at first I was afraid of what would happen, I recalled God's faithfulness to me in the past. I remembered all the other times I had delayed obedience or never obeyed and how I'd suffered for it. I also recalled the times I *had* obeyed, by His grace, and the supernatural blessing and provision that had come from His hand as a result of simply obeying His commands. You know, when we get serious about God's business, He gets serious about His blessings. It's regrettable that we are so often discouraged and depressed over the seeming lack of God's providence in our lives...when in reality, He's withholding His supernatural activity because our stubborn will chooses to disobey His clear command.

So I wrote the check. I slid the checkbook across the desk. I looked at it. My heart was racing. And I said out loud, "Okay, Lord. I did it. You're in charge now. If I bounce a check because of this, I'm just going to trust that You've got my back."

The irony of my words still staggers me! That was exactly the point! Jesus *does* have my back. He is my security. He is my safety net. He is my insurance. He is my ironclad guarantee. My faith is in Christ alone, even though sometimes I forget it.

∞

The next morning, my wife took the boys with her to run some errands and I had about three hours before lunch with our friends. I decided to go for a run. I thought it would curb some of the anxiety I was feeling about the $1000 check. As I headed out toward the six-mile loop I usually ran, I heard God speak to me again in my spirit. He said, *Clayton, you can trust Me. I will bless you for your obedience.* It sounded so real that I stopped in my tracks. Then, as I kept walking down the driveway, I heard Him speak again. No kidding. He said, *Look in your mailbox.*

This was a very strange thing for God to say. He's supposed to say things that are nobler or more epic. Like giving orders to conquer the forces of evil, issuing commands to build arks that survive a worldwide flood, or dictating plans for planting a megachurch. I'd never heard anyone say that God spoke to them about their mailbox. Besides, I never check the mailbox before I go for a run. I can't carry the mail with me for six miles.

But what was the worst that could happen? What did I have to lose? I opened the mailbox and peered in. And there, inside...was some mail.

I flipped through it and saw most of it was junk. I began to wonder if God had really told me to do this. Then I saw a very official-looking envelope. To my horror, it had been sent from the IRS. And I immediately assumed the worst—I'd probably messed up my taxes or my CPA had made a mistake, and I owed the IRS truckloads of money. They would wipe out my checking account, then seize my children and eventually take a kidney to cover what I owed. (I just amaze myself at how quickly I freak out and forget that God is in control of my life, not me.)

I thought about putting the letter back in the mailbox without opening it, but I would suffer intolerable anxiety on my run. So I reluctantly opened it.

What followed was a tidal wave of emotions beginning with disbelief, moving toward confusion, and ending with rapturous joy, as I danced on the side of the road like a six-year-old girl at her surprise birthday party.

I'd taken out the contents of the envelope and the first thing I'd seen was a check. It was made out to me. This was good, but the numbers didn't make sense. I looked at the amount and knew I'd seen it wrong. I blinked hard and looked again. Yep, same amount. I blinked, looked away, and back to the check. Still, the same amount. $7800.

Disbelief. This is not real...I'm dreaming...no way. Confusion. How could this be...they made a mistake...it was a computer error. Rapturous joy. This is a lot of money...this is awesome...wait till I tell my wife!

I again looked down at the stack of mail in my hands as I jumped up and down and noticed another official-looking envelope. This one was from the North Carolina Department of Revenue. I opened it without even pausing.

There was no check inside. Just a letter informing me that I'd been paying too much estimated tax for the past few years and the state owed me money. Within a few weeks, I would be getting a check for $2200.

> God controls the cosmos. If He needed our money, He would find a way to get it out of our greedy little hands. He doesn't want our money. He wants our hearts.

I did the math. I was getting $10,000 completely unexpectedly. Out of nowhere. And from the government! And the check and the letter were in my mailbox at the same time on the same day, the day that I was going to meet with Sarah and Rabi to give them a $1000 check for their ministry.

Within 12 hours of reluctantly writing the check for 10 times more than I'd originally planned, I had somehow been given 10 times more than the amount God called me to give. This amount was 100 times what I'd originally wanted to give.

I want to make something clear. I am in no way telling you that if you give money to some kind of ministry, God will automatically give you more money in return. That's not how it works. It's not about money at all. God doesn't need our money. He controls the cosmos. If He needed our money, He would find a way to get it out of our greedy little hands. He doesn't want our money. He wants our hearts. If we give Him our heart, then He has us completely: our loyalty, affection, finances, desires, and habits. That is why obedience is so vitally important in our relationship with Him. It shows us how much we love Him and trust Him. It also reveals how much we love our money, our stuff, and the false sense of security and identity we find in places and things other than the love God has for us. When He calls us to obey, it sometimes means abandoning conventional wisdom and taking a risk others would think insane. Yet these are the times that stretch our faith, and build our faith.

If we never take a risk for God, do we ever really trust God? Trust has to be more than a word we throw around. It must have some results.

There have been numerous other times in my life when I obeyed God and saw no miraculous results, no big checks in the mail. Yet the principle remains the same. He keeps His word. He is trustworthy. And if we can believe He created the universe, raised Jesus from the dead, and can save us from our sins, then we can trust that when He calls us to do something amazing, even though it may seem crazy to us, He has something in mind and sees the outcome. Just obey. He's got your back.

Now...listen and see if He's speaking to you. If He is, and you obey, you just may have an amazing story to tell when it's all said and done. Even if it doesn't involve the IRS.

23

Close to the Kingdom

When Jesus saw that he had answered wisely, he said to him, "You are not far from the kingdom of God." And from then on no one dared ask him any more questions.

—Mark 12:34

In the Gospels, we see Jesus establishing rapport with notorious sinners, eating with them and going to their homes. We see the same Jesus condemning religious hypocrites for their hollow self-righteousness. They based their worth on sacrifices and works. But one of the religious teachers, the one in Mark 12:34, understood that works of the flesh meant nothing. It was this heart attitude that got the attention of the Master.

The man had just told Jesus that the greatest commandment of all is to love God with everything you are and to love your neighbor as you love yourself. He said that these things mattered more to God than sacrifices and burnt offerings. When Jesus then responded that he was close to the kingdom, it was both good and bad. It was good because being close to the kingdom was better than being far away. It was bad because being close to the kingdom meant that he was still not there yet.

When I think of kingdom people, those who are actually a living part of it, names like Martin Luther, Amy Carmichael, and William Carey come to mind. But according to Jesus, there's another group in this world that is close to, but not in, the kingdom. Surrounding us every day are millions of unlikely candidates for kingdom membership and inclusion. We tend to slam the door in their faces, yet these are the very people for whom Christ died: homosexuals, drug dealers, abortionists, atheists, pedophiles, prostitutes, drunks.

> He was closer to being truly saved than thousands of churchgoers, ones who base their salvation on church attendance or denominational affiliation yet have never had a personal encounter with Christ.

They are on the outside looking in. Words like *propitiation, atonement, repentance,* and *justification* mean nothing to them. Our traditions and even our morals are foreign to their minds. We shouldn't expect them to act like us either. Why do we project our morality onto the world? There's nothing inside them that would motivate or enable them to live a morally upright life.

Scripture is crystal-clear that until people are saved and have the Holy Spirit, they will never understand who we are and how we live. Get used to it, and move on to establishing relationships with people who need the Lord.

∽

My wife and I were on vacation the summer after we were married, and as we drove the interstate I saw a man who evidently needed a ride. So we picked up this hitchhiker outside of Portland, Oregon. He had run out of gas, so when he got in the car with us, he said thanks for the lift. I took this as a chance to begin witnessing to him. I told him we followed Jesus, and I asked him if he knew Christ. (Now, this was Portland, Oregon—not Atlanta or Dallas or Nashville, where everyone you meet will tell you they're Christians because of their parents, their baptism as a kid, or their love for fried chicken.)

Instead of the same lame response I usually get from people when I ask if they know the Lord, he turned in his seat, looked me dead in the eyes, and said firmly, "No!"

I was so surprised I actually gasped! I asked him what he did believe, if anything, and he responded unapologetically that he was a pagan. He worshipped nature—rocks and trees and rivers. He didn't believe in absolute truth, and certainly not in Jesus. I asked if I could give him a Bible. "Don't bother" was his reply. As we let him out at the gas station I told him I would pray for him, and he said we shouldn't waste our time. He was honest—strikingly so.

I tell this story all over the nation to audiences of Christians, and when I share about the hitchhiker's blunt refusal to listen to me or even let me pray for him, the crowds always gasp in disbelief. They seem offended that a man would be so coldhearted. But I have to wonder, what is more offensive to God: an honest pagan or a lying hypocrite?

The last thing I said to him was that he wasn't far from the kingdom of God. He was at least willing to admit that he was lost, a non-Christian making no attempt to lie or pretend. He was closer to being truly saved than thousands of churchgoers, ones who base their salvation on church attendance or denominational affiliation yet have never had a personal encounter with Christ that brings them to their knees in humility and repentance. He was halfway to salvation. He knew he wasn't a Christian.

ஃ

Not long after we returned from Oregon, I was talking to a well-known music producer late one night at a Chinese restaurant. Out of the blue, he asked me how I'd become a Christian. After I shared my story, I asked him if he was saved. He said no. When I asked him why not, he simply said that sex with his girlfriend was more important at the moment, and he wouldn't give that up. He said he knew he deserved hell for the sins he had committed and knew he was foolish for rejecting Christ. He seemed so far away at that moment, yet was so close because he knew that coming to Christ meant denying himself. He just refused to. I told him he wasn't far from the kingdom. He at least admitted his need. There was no pretense.

∽

There was a time when you and I were also separated from God. Don't forget that you were far from the kingdom too. God can do anything—He can save you, and He can save anyone. If God loves someone, then there's hope for him or her, no matter how hopeless and far away they may seem from Him. Second Peter 3:9 tells us, "The Lord is not slow in keeping His promise, as some understand slowness. He is patient with you, not wanting anyone to perish, but everyone to come to repentance."

I think we can safely say that because of God's grace, every single person who draws breath is a little closer to the kingdom than anyone realizes. If we view people in this way instead of judging them as "outside" of salvation, then we can pray and wait in hope that God will indeed rescue them, that they will indeed repent and be saved, and that they will come to know the same peace and purpose that we do.

24

A Blind Guy in a Church Basement

The disciples were filled with joy and with the Holy Spirit.

—Acts 13:52

I HAD FINISHED MY FIRST YEAR OF COLLEGE and was single and carefree. I enjoyed the benefits of no mortgage, no car payments, and a scholarship that paid for my tuition as long as I kept up my GPA. So I filled every free moment with preaching and speaking engagements. And the summers were considerably busier than the rest of the year, even though I didn't have papers to write or classes to worry about. I would preach at youth camps all week and churches on the weekends, doing that for 12 weeks until I had to head back to college. It was on one of those Sundays that I stumbled into an amazing encounter with God that seems like it happened yesterday.

It was a small and friendly congregation in the mountains of South Carolina, and I'd preached at their morning service. I remember about a dozen people responding to the gospel, and the great fellowship I'd shared with the pastor. My parents lived only about an hour away, so I left and spent the afternoon with them and drove back to the little church for the evening service.

I arrived early because, well, that's what I was taught to do. I've always taken great care to plan my travel, to arrive before I'm supposed to, to feel settled instead of rushed, and to take my calling seriously in every respect. I usually go inside and find a quiet place to pray or meditate.

This Sunday evening I went into the church, which was still empty. I decided to roam around. The upstairs was the usual, and the downstairs was the usual, built for Sunday-school rooms. Then I found the stairs leading into the basement. Wanderlust took over. I have long been fascinated with basements, secret passageways, rooms behind closed doors, or anything out of the way that might lead to an ancient burial chamber. So I followed them down, anticipating adventure.

∞

The basement was damp and musty, and smelled old. I turned on the hall light and inquisitively wandered the corridor, cracking open every door only to find the same thing: wooden church chairs placed in small circles. Then I approached the final room on the right-hand side.

I recall that I'd felt a kind of presence in the basement when I'd stepped from the last stair, but I was unwilling to acknowledge a very tangible sense of someone else being there with me. And with the opening of every door, I convinced myself of my isolation underground. But something different awaited me in that last room.

I deliberately pushed the door back, just wide enough to step halfway in. Out of habit, I reached for the light switch to my right. Flipping it up, I experienced one of the most frightening moments of my life. As the lights chased back the damp darkness, there, on a chair in the middle of the room, sat a man. Alone and unblinking.

I shrieked with surprise, but immediately caught myself. He looked spooky. His eyes were wide open, and when the lights had illuminated the room, he hadn't blinked. I had the sensation that his eyes had been open even before there was light. I wondered if he was a zombie or a corpse; then I thought maybe I'd fallen asleep on a pew upstairs and this was a dream I was having. But he shot down all my theories when he spoke to me in a warm, gentle voice.

"Hey there. Sorry to scare you. I bet you didn't expect to see anybody down here sitting alone in the dark."

I was dumbfounded. I unleashed a nervous hiccup-hyena laugh... and then I hesitantly moved over his way. He extended his hand when I was still a good eight feet away. I quickly took it, and he shook it firmly, like old men would shake my hand at church or in town when I was with my daddy meeting his friends or business colleagues.

"I'm Brian. That was a good sermon you preached this morning." He knew it was me, but I hadn't spoken a word to him yet. I was completely freaked out.

I replied sheepishly, "Oh, you were there this morning? I love this church; the people are really friendly. And how about all those people getting saved?" There was something very peculiar about him, and I realized it was in how he looked at me...or perhaps he was looking through me.

"Yeah, that was wonderful to hear all of them getting saved. I heard it, but didn't really see it. I haven't seen anything, with my eyes at least, for years."

That was it! Brian was blind. And here he was sitting all alone in a dark classroom in the basement of the church. It was an awkward moment.

So I asked, "What are you doing down here all by yourself?"

"Well, I spend a lot of time alone. I don't have many friends now that I can't see anymore. So I get a ride to church, and I just come down here and sit in the dark by myself. The dark here doesn't bother me, because my world is always dark now. When I hear people start walking around upstairs, I know it's time for church to start, so I walk upstairs and join everybody. I don't miss many Sundays nowadays."

∞

I found myself feeling sorry for Brian, for his situation and his loneliness. I'd met blind people before, but I'd never been alone with someone who had lost their vision, especially in such an isolated location. It wasn't Brian himself that made me feel so uncomfortable; it was the flood of crazy thoughts suddenly rushing through my mind, wondering what I would do if I couldn't see anymore.

I put myself in his shoes for a moment, and I realized it would be easy to lose your mind if all of a sudden you could never see the color green again, never watch the sun set through the clouds on the western horizon, or never look at the expression on a person's face while having a deep conversation with them. That thought, along with the musty smell of the dark basement and the startling realization that a blind guy had been sitting all alone down there, gave me an unsettled feeling. My palms got sweaty.

Then Brian said, "Mr. King, step a little closer to me. I want to show you something."

That was the last thing on earth I wanted to do. What in the world did he want to show me, and why did I have to step closer to him? What if he *was* crazy? This was just weird, and I started thinking about turning around and running out of the room, down the hall, and up the stairs. Then I remembered he would eventually come upstairs too and hear me preach, and I would be embarrassed. So I reluctantly walked over.

Then he grabbed my left hand. It sent a cold chill down my spine. With a firm grip he moved it up toward his face. What in the world was this guy going to do?

He felt my tension and said in a soft tone, almost a whisper, "Don't worry, this won't hurt. I just want to explain to you how I went blind."

I relaxed, and he guided my hand all the way to his head. He placed it on his right temple, where his hairline started. He found my trigger finger, straightened it out, and rubbed it across his scalp until I felt something underneath the surface rolling around under my finger. It was small and round, but not perfectly round. I pulled my finger away, and I could see the outline of an object that shouldn't have been there.

> He spoke up, sensing I was at a loss for words. "But you know what, Mr. King? I'm so thankful all of this happened to me."

"You felt it, didn't you, Mr. King? That's why I'm blind today. I tried to kill myself here a while back. I'd gotten into some bad stuff and I wasn't thinking straight. So I took a pistol and put it up to my head. I just wanted to die so badly. I figured blowing my brains out would be the quickest way, and it was guaranteed to work.

"Boy, was I wrong. I pulled the trigger and the gun fired, but the bullet missed my brain. It went clear through the front of my head, behind my eyes, through my sinuses. It tore through all the optical nerves and the stuff that lets me taste food. I can't smell fragrances anymore either. And it stopped right under the skin on the other side. That's what you feel right there. It's the actual bullet I tried to kill myself with.

"They left it in there because they said it was lodged in a bad place filled with blood vessels and nerves. I've gotten sort of attached to it. I like to rub it and feel it because it reminds me of how low I got and how God reached down and saved me. I mean, what are the chances that you shoot yourself in the head and survive? God wanted me to live even when I didn't."

❧

I didn't know what to say to Brian. I was too overcome with emotion. In the last few minutes I'd been scared to death by a strange man sitting alone in a dark room, freaked out that he knew my name before

I ever spoke a word to him, and then blown away by hearing about his suicide attempt. I got weak in the legs and sat down in a chair beside him. The adrenaline was pumping through my body, and my hands were still sweating.

He spoke up, sensing I was at a loss for words. "But you know what, Mr. King? I'm so thankful all of this happened to me."

"Why is that, Brian?" I replied.

"Because it took all of this for me to see that I needed to change my life. People around here feel sorry for me, but I keep telling them there's nothing to feel sorry for. Most folks think that if you can't see, smell, or taste, then your life is mostly over. But I can still hear, I can still think, and I can still feel. And now that I've lost three of my senses, the ones I have left are really sharp. I use them more than a normal person would, because they are all I've got to live life with."

"Man, that is pretty incredible. It's amazing that you have such a good attitude after all that you have been through. It makes me feel convicted for ever complaining about anything."

Brian cleared his throat and shifted in his seat. "I never complain about anything anymore. When I start to feel sorry for myself, I just reach up and touch that lead slug stuck in my skull, and I remember that God gave me a second chance.

"He also gave me the best gift I could ever ask for. He gave me the vision to see His love. But He had to take away my sight to do it. It was a small price to pay.

"Because I lost my sight, but I gained eternal life."

25

Angels Speaking Swahili

Keep on loving each other as brothers. Do not forget to entertain strangers, for by so doing some people have entertained angels without knowing it.

—Hebrews 13:1-2

MY TIME IN AFRICA was one of the most significant chapters in my life. It's a continent of beauty and ferocity, where people and wild animals still live side by side, unchanged in many places for thousands of years; where the youngest and strongest are rendered weak and powerless by the tiniest creatures—unseen microbes and strange parasites.

In 1993, during my junior year in college, I flew to Nairobi, Kenya, with two close friends to minister in the villages surrounding the areas of Kakamega and Kisumu. We split up once we arrived. For several weeks I lived in a home deep in the bush with a family and their five children. I used an outhouse, slept on a wool blanket stretched over a wooden board, and bathed over a tin washtub. I could easily write an entire book just about that month in Kenya! But one of the most sacred encounters of my time there came as a result of the sickness that left me flat on my back, begging God to cure me or kill me.

I contracted malaria. I was taking every precaution, including malaria pills, and was current with all my shots, but somehow a pesky mosquito slipped the parasite into my bloodstream in one tiny bite.

I'm not exaggerating when I say that I honestly believed I would die in the jungles of Kenya.

I describe malaria this way: Imagine the worst case of flu and the hottest fever you've ever had. Now imagine being forced to sprint a mile uphill, becoming so dehydrated that you're unable to keep any water in your system no matter how fast you gulp it. You suffer hunger pains, but the thought of food makes you want to vomit; so you're unable to regain strength. Finally, all you can do is sleep, but it's not in the least restful. You're plagued by weird dreams and terrible nightmares, constantly waking up with the feeling that other people in the room want to hurt you or kidnap you in your sleep. That is malaria, or at least how it feels.

I had a good, strong case of it. And I'm not exaggerating when I say that I honestly believed I would die in the jungles of Kenya.

Have you ever felt that way before—alone, afraid, helpless? Far from home with no one to rescue you, just waiting and hoping for a miracle? It's not a sacred feeling—It's a *scared* feeling!

I lay on my makeshift bed for several days with, as I described, nothing between me and the wooden boards but a wool blanket. I was dripping with sweat one moment and freezing with chills the next. The burning fever had made me crazy—as I slipped in and out of a restless, torturous sleep I was having hallucinations. I didn't know where I was. I thought about my parents back home and longed for my mother, who could comfort and console in just about any situation. I hadn't eaten in days and was dehydrated from vomiting. It was the lowest point of my life physically.

It's deep in our nature to call on God in time of great need. It's hard-wired into us. Even the most stalwart atheists have been known to call on God when a child is diagnosed with cancer or their wife is moments away from dying in childbirth.

I certainly called on Him in that mud hut. I told God to cure me or kill me. And in the midst of my desperation, He sent angels.

Early on the fourth morning of the fever, deep in another crazy hallucination, I heard voices in the room with me. This was nothing new, but these voices were speaking a different language. It was familiar to me, but I didn't understand the words they were saying. Then the speaking became more intense. I felt people's hands all over me—on my arms, legs, and head. I thought they were carrying me away, maybe even to bury me. Maybe I had died in my sleep and angels had been sent by God to get me and take my body to the grave, or maybe to transport my soul to heaven.

What shook me out of that malarial stupor, however, was a strange heat that surged through my body. I was already burning with fever, but this was a different kind of heat—warm, electric, and soothing. The heat of the malaria was mean and hateful; this heat was peaceful and calming. I blinked a few times and realized I was indeed surrounded by angels—but not the kind you see in storybooks or movies. These angels had dark skin and were praying in Swahili.

A dozen Kenyan pastors, all of whom had heard about my sickness, had gathered to lay their hands on me and pray for my healing and restoration. Only a few of them had shoes on their feet, and one of them had walked 12 miles to get there. The 12-mile walk home remained for him—and he was one of the barefoot pastors!

I stirred and tried to get up while they held me down, telling me to rest. But they couldn't keep me in that bed! I rose to embrace each of them. God had heard my cries of desperation; He had answered my prayers and sent a small band of His special angels. I saw these men as the spiritual equivalent to the Navy SEALs, a band of brothers God had sent on an important mission to do His will. They certainly saved my life that day.

I wish every Christian could experience such an encounter with God, a sacred moment like the one I had in the jungle that day. Waking up to the peace of the Lord Jesus as brothers covered and protected me in prayer, touching my flesh with theirs, calling on God for His intervention, was one of the most holy moments in my life.

What is it that you need to cry out to God for? Are you hopeless, stuck, empty? You can't predict how God will provide for you, but you *can* trust that He hears you when you call His name. He cares for you unlike anyone else in this world. And perhaps the depth of your need will be equal to the glory He will get when He rescues you from your catastrophe.

Nothing is too hard for Him. Call on Him; He just might send angels.

26

One Voice

My sheep listen to my voice; I know them, and they follow me.

—John 10:27

My biggest struggle is being too busy to sit still and listen. I'm a very energetic and self-motivated person by nature, so I tend to pack every free moment of the day with activity. I schedule meetings and lunches and speaking engagements until I realize, at the end of the day, that I've forgotten about God altogether. This isn't just an occasional problem—if I'm not careful, it can happen to me every single day.

I feel like I live my life in a hurry, surrounded by distracting noises and sounds. I always feel rushed. As a result, I often find myself feeling frazzled and burned out. Then I get short with people, and hard to live with. But it's my own fault.

Just the other day, as I rushed out the door to catch a flight (I'm seldom early for flights; I wait until the very last minute to leave), I remember saying to myself, *God does not mean for me to live my life in a hurry like this.*

Is this resonating with you? Or am I the only one who feels this way?

A good friend of mine describes it as the "tyranny of the urgent." We don't take seriously the daily cultivation of a relationship with God, so we make excuses by saying that we just have to do certain things that are important.

> We look for God in the wrong places. American Christianity is in many ways built around big events, crusades, revivals, and concerts. We think this is where we encounter God because of the volume of religious activity.

When I do this, I'm implying that those things are more important than the Lord Jesus.

Come on now. Be honest. This is what we really mean when we rush through a day without a moment to spare for Christ. I can't listen to Him if I never take time to be still. And if I'm not in the habit of listening to Him, then when He does speak to me, I may not even recognize His voice.

What a sad way to live! But it seems to be the cultural waters that we're all forced to swim in. Everyone is busy. We never slow down. It's always loud. We are always distracted.

The psalmist tells us to be still. It's in that stillness we will be filled with the reality of God's presence and personality. It's in that stillness and quiet that God reveals Himself to us. If our lives are full of noise and distraction, we may never fully embrace the reality that He is God.

For years I've had this theory about noise. You know as well as I do that our world is just one distraction after another. So consider for a moment your habits. What's the first thing you do when you get in the car? Do you pop in a CD or hook up your MP3 player? What's the first thing you do when you get home or go to your room? Turn on music or the TV, or put on earphones?

Why is our existence so cluttered with noise? Are we afraid of silence? Maybe we know that in silence we are made aware of God and thus of our own sinfulness, which is uncomfortable and difficult to deal with. We'd rather not have our insecurities and inadequacies shown to us, so we drown out the voice of God by packing our lives with noise and activity. When I hear people say they can't stand to be still or that silence drives them crazy, I can't help but wonder what it is in their life they are afraid to face.

We look for God in the wrong places. American Christianity is in many ways built around big events, crusades, revivals, and concerts. We think this is where we encounter God because of the volume of religious activity. But we need to recall the experience of the prophet Elijah and that famous story from 1 Kings 19.

⁂

Elijah looked for God in the big noisy stuff. It doesn't get much bigger or more dramatic than a storm, an earthquake, and a fire. God was nowhere to be found within these powerful phenomena, even though Elijah sought Him there.

When God spoke in a gentle whisper, Elijah knew it was His voice.

The big dramatic events had to pass by before Elijah heard God, and the same is true for us. We needn't assume that God will always be found at big Christian events just because there's a Christian band or preacher there. Or perhaps God will speak to others there but not to you. That's fine. Don't fret—just find a quiet place and sit down and be still. In that silence you will know He is God.

In order to hear a whisper like Elijah did, one of two things must happen. Either all other noise has come and gone and there's total quiet so you can hear something as faint as a whisper. Or else you have to train your ear to tune out the noise and focus on the whisper above all the rest. The latter is by far the most likely situation, since there's very little chance that our world will ever slow down or be quiet. So we need to learn what God sounds like—so we'll be able to hear sacred words in sacred circumstances.

We need to be able to do both. We need to teach ourselves to wait on God even when He does not act or speak in the huge ways we expect. But more importantly, we need to train ourselves to listen to His still, small voice in the midst of confusion and noise. In other words, we can be still and know that He's God in a big crowd just as well as we can if we are alone on a mountaintop with no distraction.

It's a matter of familiarity. If we spend enough time listening to the Holy Spirit, we'll become familiar with His voice, and our ears will be trained to hear it above all other things.

∽

A perfect example was what happened at my college graduation. It was May 13, 1995, and about 4000 people were gathered at Gardner-Webb University in the Convocation Center. They were giving out awards, and I have to admit that I was uninterested. I just wanted to get my diploma and go eat, because I was starving. I was paying no attention at all, and I'd actually dozed off for a moment.

> We need to train ourselves to listen to His still, small voice in the midst of confusion and noise.

In the background, the man who was giving out awards seemed to be saying "blah-blah-blah," much like Charlie Brown's teacher in the TV *Peanuts* cartoons. As I was dozing, I vaguely heard him say, "And the winner of this year's Outstanding Male Graduate of the Year award is Clayton Ryan King."

I knew I needed to get up, but it was like when you first wake up. You wonder where you are and what is real and what is just a dream. Then the girl beside me elbowed me and said, "Get up there, you just won something!"

As I stumbled to my feet to receive the award, the noise of the crowd was deafening. I had friends, classmates, and family members there from everywhere, and pretty much everyone knew me. They were all screaming and yelling.

But above 4000 voices I could hear one voice clearly. It was the voice of my daddy as he yelled my name. He was crying, "All right, Big C!" That is what he always called me, and I could hear his voice above every other voice.

Was he that loud? Could my dad alone outshout thousands of people's cheers? No, of course not. But I'd lived with him for 22 years, and I'd heard that voice before...a familiar voice that stood out from all others. I knew it: It was my father, and he was proud of me.

∽

There's so much to learn here! We fail to be still and know God, and so we lack familiarity with His voice. We have difficulty discerning what is God, what is Satan, and what is us.

If you want to know the difference, practice cutting out all questionable influences and going into hiding. Retreat to the yard or the woods, or maybe your room. Find a place to steal away and be quiet. Follow the example of Jesus, who went away to quiet desert places to pray to His Father and meditate.

In your quiet place you will encounter God and sense His reality. You will learn who He is. Then, when your surroundings aren't quiet, you can retreat to your soul. And you'll be able to find that quiet place...the place where you can hear the warm, loving, familiar sound of your Father's voice.

27

Can I Go with You?

I LOVE TO HUNT. It was a tradition in my family long before I was born, and my own father passed it down to me.

And for me, it's not so much about getting the kill. It's more about being outside, listening to the woods, being quiet and undisturbed. Hunting connects me, in a special sort of way, to a primitive and primordial time in human history when things were tougher and survival depended on outwitting your prey. No kill, no food. While I'm thankful my family doesn't depend on my shooting ability for survival, I do feel a connection to our shared ancestry when I'm alone and cold in a stand of white oaks and the sun crests the horizon, burning off the fog of a chilly November morning. Few people ever get to experience that. I do it on purpose.

I know people who hate being alone. They need constant noise or companionship. I, on the other hand, enjoy solitude because I very seldom ever get any of it. Pursuing my public ministry means I'm constantly surrounded by people, and though this is wonderful, it does take its toll.

So my time in the woods is special and necessary. It allows me my own space without any intrusion from teenagers at a public school assembly. It gives me quiet without dozens of people to shake hands with or talk to after preaching at a church on Sunday morning. It gives me a change of pace. I'm not rushing to the airport to catch a flight. I'm not dragging a suitcase out the door or hoping that my Garmin knows the right way to the big event in South Georgia. I love what I do and I love people. But I want to *keep* loving people, and these days I spend by myself in the woods are what keeps me sane.

I have amazing encounters with God when I'm there. He helps and encourages me as I pray and sing and think. I feel His presence as I sit still and listen to the rhythms of the trees and the creek and the tree frogs. He meets me in the woods.

We are blessed to live out in the country with lots of land to hunt on. We settled here deliberately, hoping to instill values of hard work, humility, and respect for the land in our boys. I also want to pass along the tradition of respecting life and nature to my children by teaching them how to hunt legally and ethically, sharing with them how the human race sustained itself in the past by relying on the land and the animals that lived there. And I've been looking forward to the time when my boys will be old enough to join me on my trips to the woods, where just like me and my daddy, we'll talk about life and girls and sports, and make memories together that we'll share until I pass away and they pass the same traditions on to their boys, or girls, one day.

For me, time outside is about connecting. It's about me connecting with the God I love and need so desperately. It's also about me, as a little boy, connecting to manhood—because it was during those times outside that I connected most intimately with my own father. And how I love to be outside with my own boys, riding the four-wheeler or swimming in the Broad River on a hot August day! We connect, and that's what I'm trying to accomplish.

∞

Thanksgiving morning of 2009, long before anyone was up, I slipped into my camos, made a pot of coffee, and prepared for another morning of solitude in the deer stand. My entire family was still sound asleep, warm and cozy in their beds. And here I was, about to go outside and freeze for three hours while they dreamed away. But my mind was already fantasizing about watching daylight break through the darkness. I knew where the sun would crest the trees. I was imagining the giant ten-point buck that would step out in front of me.

> I remembered the exact feeling I had when my daddy told me I could come with him. It was a flood of warmth and joy unlike anything I'd ever known.

I'd been so busy for the past couple of weeks that I'd had very little time alone to just be still and quiet. But that was about to change. No one would find me in the woods. I'd be able to connect with God and listen for His still small voice. No phone calls. No e-mails. No Facebook or Twitter.

∞

As I stood in the kitchen pouring hot coffee in a thermos, I heard the thump of little feet hitting the floor. If you're a parent, you know that sound of little footsteps. You also know you can tell which of your children it is. All of a sudden Jacob, my seven-year-old, came out of his room, still in his pajamas, rubbing his eyes. I had tried to be quiet and not wake him, but he's a light sleeper—and nearly every morning he wakes up when I do, just to come sit on my lap while I read or eat or spend time with the Lord. Those are some of the most meaningful times in my life. It's when my boy and I really connect.

He saw what I was doing and began talking to me in a whisper, so as not to wake up anyone else in the house.

Jacob: Daddy, I just wanted to say good morning and I hope you get a big one today.

Me: Thanks, buddy—I appreciate that.

Jacob: Is it cold outside?

Me: Yep, pretty cold and foggy this morning.

Jacob: Okay, well, I love you, and I hope you get a big buck.

Me: Thanks, Jacob, I'll be back soon.

Jacob: Hey, Daddy—can I go with you?

I cannot even describe what my heart felt when he asked me that question. Immediately I was drawn back to my childhood, when my daddy would get up before the sun rose and I wanted to go with him so bad. He would be tying his boots. I would get his coffee, but I knew I was too little or that he wouldn't do any good hunting with me along. Until I finally got up the courage to ask if I could go. And his words filled me with hope and excitement and fear and energy. I thought of my daddy and how he had answered me. So I looked at Jacob and made his day.

"Of course you can go with me, son—I would love for you to come with me this morning!"

The look on his face was worth the world to me! With that one sentence, my little boy became a man in his own mind. He was going to join his daddy, the center of his universe, on a hunting trip! It was going to be just the two of us, together all day long, talking like boys and having adventures and seeing things in the woods. And when I looked into my son's face as he beamed from ear to ear, I remembered the exact feeling I had when my daddy told me I could come with him. It was a flood of warmth and joy unlike anything I'd ever known. I didn't call it connecting back then. I just knew I loved being with my daddy.

You see, of all the reasons I love to hunt, the one thing that makes it so enjoyable is that it was something I learned from my daddy. It was something we did together. We were big buddies in the truck and in the woods and when eating lunch on the tailgate of his old F-100 pickup. We shared those experiences, and now we remember and relive them. My daddy can't hunt anymore. He can barely even walk. So now in his old age, with diabetes and heart disease, his best days on this earth are behind him. When my dad and I talk, we talk about those days together…where we hunted and what we ate and how much it rained. I'm not making any new memories with my daddy. All I have is what we made together when I was young and he invested in me.

But *I* can still hunt. I'm young and strong and willing, and I have a son who wants to go with me. So I'm going to invest in him, in both of my boys, the same way my daddy invested in me. We'll get up early. We'll put on our boots and pack a lunch. We'll load up the old pickup truck and we'll watch the sun rise together. And it may rain us out. It may snow us in. We may not kill a single deer or squirrel. We may not kill anything but time. But is there a better way on this earth to kill time than to pass it with the people you love and cherish the most? These are the people who will be with me when I'm old and sick and unable to get out into the woods like I used to. And when that day comes, we'll have stories to tell about the good days in the woods because we took the time to be together.

The beauty of life, maybe its most tangible miracle, is that we as God's children get to do things together. We share trips and events and stories and meals with the people we love.

The beauty of life, maybe its most tangible miracle, is that we as God's children get to do things together. We share trips and events and stories and meals with the people we love. When we are old, like my daddy, we hold on to those memories, and they get us through the hard days and long nights. I will make time to take my son with me whether we kill anything or not. I will go to my boys' soccer games and baseball practices regardless of how tired I am from traveling. I will attend their school plays, I will eat lunch with them at school, and I will watch that kids' show or that movie with them, even if I'm not the least bit interested in it. I don't have to be interested in the activity. I just need to be interested in my kids.

∽

So we launched out into the cold, shivering morning air. We trudged across the wet grass, feeling our way toward the deer stand. Jacob reached up and held my hand as we walked. A rooster crowed in the distance. I was with my son.

No, we didn't kill anything that morning. And we only stayed in the stand for an hour. Even though Jacob wore three shirts, two coats, a ski mask and gloves, and even though he was wrapped up in two blankets and was sitting in my lap, his little seven-year-old body was just not used to that kind of cold. He started shivering uncontrollably, and even though he promised me he wasn't cold at all, I convinced him I was. I took the hit.

So we headed home. But I had taught him to be still, to be quiet, to watch the trail where the deer cross, and to listen to the woods. If he wants to go next time, great. If he decides hunting is not his thing, that's all right too. So long as we live our lives together, share experiences, and create stories and memories that we'll cherish when we're old men, I will be happy.

∽

As I reflect back on that morning with my son, I'm staggered at how much love God must feel for us! If I felt overwhelming joy at the idea of my son wanting to spend a morning with me in a deer stand, how much more joy does God feel when we decide to turn off the TV and sit at His feet for a while reading His Word? What does God feel like when we lift our voices together and raise our hands to Him in worship? What does it do to God's heart when I'm hurting and confused and I talk to Him and tell Him I need His help? Just like a good dad would never turn away his child in need, our good God will never turn His back on us. He loves us with an everlasting love that we cannot even comprehend. We just have to receive it and enjoy it.

Take time today, and every day, to speak to your heavenly Father. Tell Him you love Him—sing to Him and pray to Him and thank Him for how good He's been to you. It will bless Him as much as it blesses you. He loves having those moments with us, and we need those moments with Him more than anything else.

28

Going Home

Where your treasure is, there your heart will be also.

—Matthew 6:21

So there I was: wringing wet with sweat, out of breath, hot, tired, and homesick. I'd just spent over nine hours on an airplane from Zurich to Washington, DC, and now all I wanted to do was get on that flight to Charlotte. But there were 33 other people with me, and we were late for our connection. I'd just run ahead of the pack in a full sprint, yelling to the ticket agents to hold the plane to Charlotte.

I'd been in Greece and Turkey for 11 days, and I hadn't seen my pregnant wife since I'd left.

I could make that flight. I *had* to make that flight! And if that meant running through the airport screaming at strangers in order for the whole group to make this flight too, then I'd do it. Why? Because I wanted to go home.

Now don't get me wrong. Athens was an incredible city, rich in history, and the sites of Philippi, Corinth, and Ephesus overwhelmed me.

And I loved the Greek food. But once we left all that behind, my excitement began to build.

It wasn't because I love flying—I've done that for over 20 years. It wasn't because I love airplanes—they're just a means to an end. And it wasn't quality time with friends that had me excited—I'd just spent 11 days with them. It was the destination I was looking forward to.

Everyone wanted to go home. It felt so close that I could almost see the porch light. I could smell the kitchen. I could feel the cool, clean bedsheets as I slid my feet under the blankets. I knew the airplane wasn't my destination and the airport wasn't my house, so I wouldn't be satisfied until I arrived at my real home.

Have you ever been so tired and homesick that you could think of nothing else? Why is home that place we gravitate toward—not just physically, but in our hearts and minds? I believe it's because home is the most sacred place on earth.

As we age, home is the one thing our hearts need the most—a sacred space we know and are familiar with, filled with the people and images and memories that make us who we are.

Home is where we spend most of our days. It's where we have the encounters and conversations that mold us and make us think. It's where we share meals with the people we care about most on this earth. It's where funny things happen, where we laugh with each other and at each other. It's where our memory banks are filled. We yearn for home when we're away from it because it's that place of all places...where our dreams come true...where the messy arguments and tragedies of life happen.

And as we age, home is the one thing our hearts need the most—a sacred space we know and are familiar with, filled with the people and images and memories that make us who we are.

Jesus didn't own a home, or at least this is what He implied when

He said He had no place to lay His head. His home was with His disciples during His earthly ministry and with His Father in eternity. Jesus never put great worth, or value, on external things. He consistently drew people's attention back to the heart, and He did that when He talked about laying up earthly or heavenly treasure.

Christ knew that a person's heart will always lead to their treasure, because the heart is where we treasure and keep the things we love and cherish. And home is where the heart is, right?

∽

So why was I so anxious to get home? This wasn't my first international trip. I'd been away from home for more than a month on numerous occasions, backpacking in the Himalayas, living out of a tent, going weeks without a hot bath or real food. I wasn't homesick then. Once I spent a month in India leading a team of 15 students on a mission trip to one of the largest orphanages on earth. I never missed home. I had lived in Africa, India, Russia, and Jamaica—sometimes with no friends, no classmates, no one to talk to that understood me—and I'd never missed home like I did as I ran through the airport trying to get a plane to wait for us. So what made the difference?

It's not my house that I love. I'm a guy, and all I really need in order to survive is a kitchen, a bed, and a bathroom. Wood floors, wallpaper, and decorations do not do it for me like they do for my wife. It wasn't the driveway, the television, the office, or even my dogs that I missed. No, it was the peace and comfort I feel at home because home is where my treasure is.

My treasure is my wife and my boys and the memories we've made in that home: my chair where I read the Bible; my books and journals that remind me of my growth in Christ. That's what Jesus meant, and I was finally understanding it. My treasure is at home, but my treasure is not my home.

Paul the apostle understood this. He grasped it. He lived it. He wrote it. He told young Timothy that he was ready to die because he had finished the job. He also tells him that Christ is waiting in heaven to give him a crown of righteousness. Paul's destination was certain, and he looked forward to it because his treasure was Christ. That was where his heart was.

Paul would have no more wanted to stay here on earth than I would have wanted to sit in the airplane after it landed in Charlotte! Especially when I knew that my wife was waiting for me outside. She is my treasure, and my heart kept going back to her over and over again.

> I hope...we won't be dragged into the pits when momentary afflictions attack us in mind or body. When this fallen world crowds and presses in on us, may we dream of home—a home of absolute beauty and perfection.

If Christ is our treasure, then we'll think of our heavenly home in relation to Him. It's not about mansions of gold, or angels, or halos, or harps. It's *Jesus*—He's the destination and the treasure. In his most famous work, *Confessions,* Augustine summed up this thought when he said of God, "You have made us for Yourself, and our hearts are restless until they find their rest in You."

We'll do anything to get home. I've driven five or six hours late at night and early into the morning after a speaking engagement just to sleep in my own bed. We love home because the people there love us and understand us. We're accepted for who we are, and it's where we belong. We feel safe and secure.

Our eternal home will be that same thing on a perfect scale, even for those of us whose earthly home was never what it should have been. It will be a place made just for us, ruled and reigned over by the Lord Jesus.

Still, the journey is a blast. Like Paul, I don't scorn the trip here on earth. I see God's hand in every victory and defeat, every setback and bump in the road. But I can understand Paul's heart. We are not of this world; we don't belong to this world. It's offered me a few joys and pleasures, but like C.S. Lewis said, it's just a place of shadows. Earth is a shadow of reality and eternity.

In bringing this book to a close, I've stopped hundreds of times, trying to choose the right words in order to say the right things and convey the right thoughts. And as I think of going home, I guess what I really look forward to is being able to finally rest. That is it. That's what I want to do. I want to rest, knowing that Christ is my Protector, Savior, and Lord. He will allow me to lay down my burdens, never to grieve again. Hallelujah! I can only dream about that.

On this earth, I find myself feeling fatigued. I feel like Bilbo Baggins, the old hobbit in J.R.R. Tolkien's Lord of the Rings. He said he felt like "butter scraped over too much bread." I know how that feels. I also feel like Frodo Baggins, Bilbo's nephew, who was weighed down by his burden, the evil ring that had to be destroyed in the fires of Mount Doom. The closer he got to the mountain, the heavier became his burden. Not every day is like that for me, but all it takes is one day laden with sorrow, stress, or heaviness of heart to remind me of how sweet heaven is going to be.

So I pray that we'll be investing ourselves in eternity, keeping our treasure there. I hope that our hearts will gravitate toward Christ and His promise of eternal life—that we won't be dragged into the pits when momentary afflictions attack us in mind or body. When this fallen world crowds and presses in on us, may we dream of home—a home of absolute beauty and perfection. Let's dream about our encounter with Jesus, the resurrected Lord, as He stands and welcomes us. Just a few words out of His mouth and we will know that it was all worth it.

Oh, by the way...we made the flight—we made it home. And home never felt so good. But I'm guessing that one day my mind will be changed, when I reach my eternal home. It's bound to be even better than the one I live in down here.

A Word from Clayton About Crossroads Worldwide...

In 1995, I began a nonprofit ministry out of my college dorm room called Crossroads. It began with my preaching ministry and now includes multiple layers of ministry that stretch all around the world.

- *Summer camps.* Several thousand middle- and high-school students come from all over the United States every summer to our Crossroads summer camps, where they hear teaching and preaching from God's Word and participate in group activities, sports tournaments, corporate worship, and community missions.
- *Student conferences.* Every January during Martin Luther King Jr. weekend, we host a three-day conference for middle- and high-school students, as well as a separate conference for college students and young adults.
- *Mission trips.* We send short-term volunteer teams to India, Malaysia, Haiti, the Navajo reservation in Arizona, and various other places to share the gospel. We also support a full-time volunteer couple in the Himalayas as they assist in running a Christian hospital.
- *Community discipleship home.* We host two intensive discipleship programs for people ages 18 to 25, one in Boiling Springs, North Carolina (a 12-month program) and one in Manali, North India (a 6-month program).
- *Preaching ministry.* I travel full-time, teaching and preaching on evangelism, discipleship, missions, and relationships. I speak at conferences, colleges, churches, retreats, concerts, and public schools. I began this ministry at age 14 and have preached in 45 states and 30 countries to over 2 million people.

- *Writing.* In addition to the numerous books I've written, I consistently write about issues that face Christians, pastors, leaders, parents, and spouses on my blog at www.claytonking.com.
- *Media.* I have dozens of audio and video sermons online for free. Find them at

www.claytonking.com
www.newspring.cc
www.liberty.edu
iTunes: "clayton king live" or "clayton king"

For more information or to schedule one of our speakers, contact us at

www.crossroadsworldwide.com
crossroadsworldwide@gmail.com
704-434-2920

Also by Clayton King

Dying to Live

Abandoning Yourself to God's Bold Paradox

Do you want to *live?* Do want to be sold out to something that will outlive you and outlast your existence? Then you have to die. It's the only way to gain life. The only way to fill that deep-inside longing. The only way to really know Christ—because it's *His* way.

Clayton King shares 20 bold pictures from Scripture, his own life, and the lives of others that will

- make you sick of existing just to get more stuff, money, and "success"
- grip your soul with longing for the life Jesus promised
- stir up your passion for God's mission to build a kingdom that will last forever

"You wake up to a world filled with colors and tastes and textures and conversation and songs and laughter, a world that no longer revolves around your own petty drama but around God's bigger story of rebuilding what we have all broken."

Be Transformed— and Transform Your World— with These Harvest House Resources

The Unshakable Truth

How You Can Experience the 12 Essentials of a Relevant Faith

Josh McDowell and Sean McDowell

As a Christian, you may feel unsure about what you believe and why. Maybe you wonder if your faith is even meaningful and credible.

Unpacking 12 biblical truths that define the core of Christian belief and Christianity's reason for existence, this comprehensive yet easy-to-understand handbook helps you discover

- the foundational truths about God, his Word, sin, Christ, the Trinity, the church, and six more that form the bedrock of Christian faith
- how you can live out these truths in relationship with God and others
- ways to pass each truth on to your family and the world around you

Biblically grounded, spiritually challenging, and full of practical examples and real-life stories, *The Unshakable Truth* is a resource applicable to every aspect of everyday life. *Study guide avaible.*

BECOMING WHO GOD INTENDED

DAVID ECKMAN

Whether you realize it or not, your imagination is filled with *pictures* of reality. The Bible indicates these pictures reveal your true "heart beliefs"—the beliefs that actually shape your everyday feelings and reactions to family, friends, and others, to life's circumstances, and to God.

David Eckman compassionately shows you how to allow God's Spirit to build new, *biblical* pictures in your heart and imagination. As you do this, you will be able to accept God's acceptance of you in Christ, break free of negative emotions and habitual sin...and finally experience the life God the Father has always intended for you.

"I strongly urge you to get Becoming Who God Intended *and put it to work in your life."*

—JOSH MCDOWELL

I Can't See God...Because I'm in the Way

Getting Beyond Self-Centered Religion to a Passionate Faith

Bruce Bickel and Stan Jantz

If you're stuck in your Christian faith and can't figure out why, you may be missing the obvious—your own "belief behaviors." Steering clear of cliché solutions, authors Bruce Bickel and Stan Jantz help you uncover how, when, and where you could be getting in your own way, hindering yourself from the experience of a transforming, heart-igniting faith. They invite you to

- consider God's big plan and how you can join what He's doing in the world
- commit to follow God's wisdom rather than disregard it
- relinquish control so you can embrace God's leading and purpose for you

This honest soul search will inspire you and make you think...so you can replace belief boredom with hunger for God's truth and the desire to renew your mind and spirit.